PRAISE FOR BETTER THAN JESUS

In his previous book, *The Holy Spirit is Not a Bird*, Ty attempts to take any preconceived weirdness out of the baptism of the Holy Spirit and illustrates how the work and person of the Holy Spirit is normal for all Christians. In his latest work, *Better than Jesus*, he builds on that premise and challenges believers to embrace John 16. Believers who desire a fully Spirit-empowered life must listen and respond to the Spirit's guidance!

–Doug Clay, General Superintendent,
Assemblies of God

"With humor and wit, Ty deftly navigates the waters of theological discourse to provide practical insight into a more fully Trinitarian experience. Behind the provocative title lies authentic pastoral guidance on what it means to be Spirit-led à la John 16. While avoiding the pitfalls of many self-help manuals, this book raises important questions about what it means to live as a Christian in the world today.

–Terance Espinoza, Ph.D., Professor of Bible and Theology,
Southwestern Assemblies of God University.

Ty Buckingham knows the heart and voice of the Holy Spirit; this book will take you deeper into both.

–Tim Enloe, Author and Conference Speaker,
Enloe Ministries

· TY BUCKINGHAM ·

Published by Oliver Royal Publishing

Cover design by Joshua Noom

Edited by Candice Tyer, LLC.

International Standard Book Number:
978-0-578-68212-9

Library of Congress Catalog Card Number Pending.

For Rebecca, the best is still yet to come.

BETTER THAN JESUS

CONTENTS

BETTER THAN JESUS

Jesus Is Amazing

First off, I know a title like *Better Than Jesus* can be a tad misleading, but the truth you will find in this book is that it's not misleading but leading you to what you've missed. Jesus, by a wide margin, is the most amazing thing in my life. He gave me the life I have.

If you don't have a relationship with Jesus yet, I would encourage you to put this book down and get that before you try to get into this book. I wrote this book to push and stretch you, as Jesus has done with me. If you don't have Jesus in your life, I love you enough to tell you to put this down and find Him before anything else. Once you've done that, I've got you.

I had an interesting journey to finding Jesus and being

what the Bible would call "born again." I lived most of my childhood having a nominal Christian experience: going to church, praying for what I wanted, and obligatorily reading my Bible after I'd negotiated with God that I would. (As a kid, whenever using the bathroom was taking a while, I promised that if He would hurry things up, I'd read my Bible every day …)

Once I got real about Jesus' realness, everything in my life changed. My relationships, finances, opportunities, and heart experienced a shift that I can only regard as supernatural. Nothing was too crazy growing up. To this day, I have never smoked or consumed alcohol, and I didn't have sex before marriage (still don't know if that was by choice or not but, hey, it worked out). Even though my life didn't necessarily look different right away, the change was very real. Finding out that Jesus didn't just love who I was going to be but loved who I already was really messed me up in the best way.

From high school onward I started to go after Jesus in a very intentional way, and it was working well for me. Then I had a moment when I was really introduced to Holy Spirit. I wasn't at a youth camp or church service, either. I found Holy Spirit in a relational way in a college dorm room. I began praying for hours every night, trying to get closer to Him, pursuing what it looked like to have relationship with Him. I ended up realizing that there was something more than just Jesus, and it was also from Jesus.

Since starting my relationship with Holy Spirit, which has turned into what I would consider friendship, the miraculous has become my new normal in the most normal way. I don't have to make anything up or conjure any sort of emotional response. Holy Spirit simply moves because of the relationship I have with Him. People's lives are changed on a regular basis not because of who I am but because of who I have. We can all see miracles on a regular basis, and we don't have to be weird about it.

This book is about what Jesus says is better for us. He calls it a gift, which means we don't have to beg for it. This gift has your name on it and, just like any other gift, all you have to do is receive it.

This book is not for the spiritual elite. It was written for normal people who want to live an amazing life. It's meant to open our eyes to the very thing that is right in front of us, the thing Jesus is trying to show every human on Earth.

BETTER THAN JESUS

Walmart Miracles

I hadn't prayed for more than five minutes before I got to Walmart. Saying it like that makes it sound as if I need to be prayed up to go to Walmart, and that's not the case. I woke up and prayed while I got ready, which, honestly, probably takes me 10 minutes total on a typical day. While in the shower, I pray and sing a song from my shower playlist—judge me, but it's about the same as the average teenage girl's workout playlist.

I was getting ready to fly out the next day to speak at a conference when I realized I didn't have any toiletries to travel with me. I had forgotten to check the bathroom one last time before I left my hotel days before, so I needed to run to the store to get a few items for my trip and for our house. The list consisted of deodorant, a dollar

toothbrush (okay, I hate bringing my electric toothbrush
anywhere, so I buy cheap ones and throw them away
when I check out of my hotel when traveling), laundry
soap and, if I remembered, my wife's favorite cereal. I
had accidentally eaten the last of it.

Let's get a couple things straight, though. First, I should
know better than to eat the last bowl of another human's
cereal. Clearly, this was a low point in my life. Second,
it was a regretful cereal at that: Honey Bunches of Oats.
Don't get me wrong. I don't think it's an inherently bad
cereal; I just feel it's a cereal pretending to be healthier
than it is. I eat Cocoa Puffs and I'm cool with that choice,
because I'm not pretending to be healthy. I know … I'm
just not getting over the fact that I'm an adult.

Does all of this matter? It does. Hang on.

It turns out that my wife, Rebecca, is busy in the office,
so I end up taking this trip to the store by myself. The
drive is nothing extraordinary, some talk radio with a
mix of a couple songs I shuffle through. I park the car
in the first spot I see and begin to make my way into
Walmart. This is when things get interesting.

I start walking from my car into the store and, all of a
sudden, I feel this nudge. That's the best way I can describe how it feels when Holy Spirit speaks—like a
nudge in the right direction. Nothing physical happens;
it often comes as a thought. Most people, me included,
hear from God in our thoughts, which is why you need

to be aware of your thought life. It's the same place you'll hear God's voice. If your thoughts aren't clean, distinguishing God's voice from your thoughts may be hard for you. Let me give you an example. I work from home most days. We have an office, but I almost always work from the couch in our living room. I have to understand that it has two purposes: work and live. When my wife is home, that space is no longer my office but our home, so I keep it clean at all times. Our thoughts are the same way. We need to regularly clean and purify them so that when Holy Spirit shows up at random, we'll be able to welcome Him. We won't have to go through the process of second-guessing whether or not we hear His voice.

So, the nudge happens. Unlike normal, I feel Holy Spirit tell me something oddly specific. It feels like a best friend giving me a harder-than-usual nudge and almost pushing me off a chair. I'm about to walk into Walmart when I hear Holy Spirit:

"You can't leave Walmart until you heal the sick."

Can I be real with you? The first thing that came to my mind was, "Can we chill out Holy Spirit? That's a little heavy." I'm being totally honest. Why? Because I am a normal human being. I didn't doubt God, but I felt the weight of what I was being called to do.

Into Walmart I go.

The double doors open. (To this day, even if I don't do it

physically, I pretend my powers are what open the door. If you don't do this at least once a week, you're lost.)

I walk into the store feeling this nudge from Holy Spirit to heal the sick, which is an interesting phrase on its own. When we see Jesus doing anything, it is the representation of God's character. When we see Holy Spirit, we see an impartation of God's power into Jesus and into those who have been born again. When reading the Word, I don't often see Jesus saying, "Go and pray for the sick," but rather, "Go and heal the sick." In this moment, I could feel Holy Spirit nudging me to do the same.

At this point, I have two options. I can be my normal self, who Jesus uses out of love, favor, and some crazy mix of anointing that He has placed on me. Or I can be super weird. The weird guy is someone who walks into Walmart and starts asking every single human being, "Can I pray for you?" Now, is there anything wrong with that? Maybe. I'm all for evangelism; however, there is power when we are ourselves in these moments. God doesn't need you to become someone different in order for something to change. God is calling who you are in Jesus to be the difference so someone else can change.

When Holy Spirit speaks and tells me to pray for someone, I believe He will also tell me who that person is. This isn't some kind of strange scavenger hunt where Holy Spirit is playing games with me and someone else. Too often we have this poor belief that Holy Spirit is trying to test us to see how spiritual we are. Does that occur? For sure. One hundred percent, there are seasons and moments when He pushes us. But we often think something is a test when it's really a testament to who Holy Spirit is through us. Why would He tell me to pray for the sick and leave me alone to figure out who He's talking about? The worst-case scenario is I'd have to spend an hour trying to hunt the person down, asking everyone I see if they're sick—all before the person I'm supposed to pray for leaves Walmart. I choose to be myself, and you should too.

I grab a shopping cart and start getting what I need. I pass by the pharmacy to the beauty section and grab deodorant, a toothbrush, and some travel-size toothpaste. In this moment, I realize I only need to get two more things. I'm pushing this cart, looking like the laziest human who can't hold three things. I get the detergent we need and prepare to leave. Notice that nothing of biblical proportions or noteworthy has happened yet. But it's about to get really good.

I start heading to the front of the store where there are what looks like countless checkout lanes, but only two are actually open. (Can I get a witness up in here?) I'm about halfway toward the front of the store when I feel another nudge. Again, I feel nothing physical and hear no audible sounds. It came as a prompt, or thought, that seemed to be Holy Spirit. I feel Him say, "In three aisles from now is the one who you need to heal."

Holy Spirit tells me that the person I am supposed to

pray for is three aisles down from where I am. I have the two options of either moving forward toward what I feel could be Holy Spirit, or I can turn the other way and avoid any possibility of being wrong (or right).

My biggest regrets have come from walking the wrong way. Once when I felt I was supposed to pray for someone, I ended up walking the opposite way because I was afraid of being wrong. After feeling like I'd missed it, I tested God (not advisable) and said, "I don't know. Maybe that wasn't even really You. If it was, give me a sign in the next five seconds." I looked over to my left and saw a magazine stand. I kid you not—the magazine at the very top was TIME, and Jesus' face was on the cover. (I couldn't even make that up!) Was it a coincidence? Maybe. But I think God uses coincidences to convict and convince us.

I step out in faith and continue moving forward this time.

Aisle one. I look down the aisle, sheepishly hoping I don't see anyone. Nobody. Thank you, Jesus.

Now, this isn't happening when I'm initially getting to know Jesus. This is me as a professional speaker who talks about Jesus. The truth is: I still hate awkward moments. I'm working on it.

Aisle two. I look down the aisle and, once again, no one's there. My heart starts to beat a little faster and I start getting a little nervous, which is usually a sign that I'm on the right track.

Aisle three. I look and see the most powerful thing. There is a sale on Cocoa Puffs! You might be thinking, "How could you be thinking of cereal?" Can we be honest? If a miracle is going to happen in Walmart, it's going to happen in the cereal aisle. I have never seen water turn into wine, but I have seen milk turn into chocolate milk, and that is a straight up miracle.

The aisle is occupied by only one other person—a woman who is a Walmart employee. Of course, with the Holy Spirit nudging me more and more that she is the one to pray for, I set my mind to what is important. I grab two boxes of Cocoa Puffs. (Don't even pretend like you wouldn't do the same.)

The lady then looks at me and asks, "Do you need help with anything?" I mean, she is technically asking for it at this point, right? I walk up to her with all calmness and sobriety, and I take a real step into the nudge of Holy Spirit. "Hey, yeah, this might be super weird (because it probably is for someone who may have never had a moment with Jesus like this before), but I have a relationship with God. I think He is super real and I'm trying to hear His voice better, and I just have this feeling that I am supposed to pray for you. Would that be okay?"

WOULD THAT BE OKAY?

I think those are the four most powerful words you can say when praying for someone. I don't want to just be some weirdo who sees someone who needs prayer and, at the top of my lungs while running toward them, yells, "IN THE NAME OF JESUS, I DECLARE YOU ARE FREE!" That might make a good movie scene, but it can create a lot of unnecessary baggage in me and the person getting ministered to.

You might think that never happens, but I see it all the time when people are praying for others. They turn into someone else, some old school preacher who has to yell in order for Jesus to hear them. When has yelling made anything better in any relationship? Never. So, don't yell. Don't be who you think you're supposed to be. Be yourself and Jesus will take care of the rest.

I ask the woman if I can pray for her and she says, "I don't see why not." (For the record, she was getting paid, and someone praying for you while you're getting paid isn't a bad deal.) As I am about to pray for her, I feel another nudge from Holy Spirit. "Back. Seven years." This is what is called a word of knowledge, which is when God gives a believer information in order to help someone else understand that God knows them and their situation. The goal in this moment is not for her to see that I am spiritual but to see that God sees her—so much that He, the God of the universe, would use a random guy to interrupt her life.

I say, "This might be crazy also, but do you have any

back issues from something from, like, seven years ago?" Immediately, tears start rolling down her face. I've made some women cry before, but this time is different. In this moment, this woman experiences the living God in a powerful way, probably for the first time ever. After she composes herself, she says, "Yes."

I then find out she has been, and is currently, in severe back pain from an incident that took place over seven years prior. This is when everything shifts. This is when it moves from me in my faith and obedience to Jesus truly showing off. Miracles are the easiest part of my life because I don't do them. Jesus does them through me so that I can't take credit.

With my hands in my pockets, I pray for her in the middle of Walmart's cereal aisle. "God, You love my friend Sarah (name changed), and You love her so much that You died for her and made a way for her to have life in her and healing upon her. So, I pray that You would heal my friend." The woman looks at me, moves her shoulders around, moves her back from side to side, and begins to weep. In between her tears and laughter, she tells me that she has never felt so good in her entire life. "I think your God just healed me."

This is one of the countless stories I have to tell. That might sound like the most arrogant statement ever, but hold on. I have countless stories, and you can too. This isn't my story; this is a Kingdom story. If you believe Jesus is Lord, then you have been given the ability to do amazing things like this with Holy Spirit.

Have you ever wondered why Jesus left us Holy Spirit? Have you ever wondered if there were more to your life than just being saved? There is more than you have ever experienced, seen, or wondered. God is about to drop something in your soul in a way that will change you forever.

In this book, we are going to examine biblical truths, observing what Jesus talked about and what He wants to give us, all while experiencing what happens when we receive the very thing Jesus said is better. We will discover what is better for us, how we take advantage of the advantage we are given, and what that means for every believer in Jesus moving forward. What's the best part about it? Jesus is the one who provides it.

REFLECTIONS

When is the last time you did something for the first time with Holy Spirit?

_____

_____

_____

_____

_____

What would have to happen in order for you to believe you could see a miracle?

_____

_____

_____

_____

_____

When you think of Holy Spirit, what is the first thing that comes to mind?

_____

_____

_____

_____

_____

BETTER THAN JESUS

Better Than Jesus

Life is better without Jesus.

I know that may sound crazy, but Jesus says so Himself. Isn't it fascinating that every great story of Jesus involves Him getting to a person—or a person pushing through crowds, breaking down roofs, even breaking laws, all to get a moment with Him? Those narratives have incredible value, but what if we didn't have to push through, break down, or disobey a law to get to what Jesus has? We can relate to these stories, but there is a part of us that doesn't want to just relate anymore. There is a part begging for us to get healed, to touch Jesus' clothes—no more climbing a tree to get a good view. We don't have to wait or push to get to Jesus, and it's way better this way. It's better for humanity.

When we look at the life of Jesus, we see one major goal: for us to be in relationship and right standing with God the Father and get into the Kingdom of God. It's such a beautiful paradox that the one person to never have a biological father was the one getting us to our heavenly Father. Jesus' goal was not just to save you from your past life but to give you a brand new one, to give you the opportunity to be born once again. Jesus was constantly doing things so that we would see that He is the only way to God.

Jesus was confined to the same kind of earthly body as you and me. This is what the term "incarnation" is referring to, that Jesus put on skin and bone so He could live a life no one could live and die a death no one could die—a death that covered all past and present sin.

In His human body, Jesus was limited to being in one place at one time. Yes, there were monumental moments when Jesus healed people who were in another town. Even then, someone had to get to Jesus in order for Him to know to do the miracle. The greatest stories of Jesus we read about in the Bible, heard preached, or read about in other books written about Him all have to do with the human factor. A human was trying to get something from God, so they had to get to Jesus in His earthly body. This was all the divine setup for what Jesus says at the end of the story, the end of His time physically on the earth. After 33 years and countless miracles and deep friendships, Jesus says something astonishing: "It's better that I leave."

JESUS' UN-FAMOUS LAST WORDS

"It is finished." (John 19:30)

When we think of the last words Jesus spoke, many of us go straight to His last words on the cross. However, while the last words He ever spoke on earth may not be more powerful, they are empowering.

It's quite humorous to think that many believe Jesus' last words are, "It is finished." What's funny to me is that His last words are actually the exact opposite. They are all about the beginning of something new, receiving something new. The last thing Jesus says is that we should receive Holy Spirit. These are the last recorded words of Jesus, and it's been 2,000 years since.

"But you will receive power when the Holy Spirit comes upon you; and you will be my witnesses in Jerusalem, and in all Judea and Samaria, and to the ends of the earth." After he said this, he was taken up before their very eyes, and a cloud hid him from their sight. (Acts 1:8-9)

Jesus leaves the scene with this. Right before He gives a command to His people, He says in Acts 1:4 to go and wait to receive the gift that the Father promised. He then talks about how we are not just to be baptized (or immersed) in water to show our salvation. We are to also be baptized in the Holy Spirit, immersed with power to not just be saved but to save others. More on that later.

Imagine that the last thing Jesus says to you after being with you for years is to go wait for something that has never been seen. Think of Noah building an ark for rain that has not yet come. Heavy rain had never come from the sky, but he is building an ark to house something for the next generation and, really, the new world. Jesus does the same thing. He tells us that we are now the housing. Jesus may not use the word "ark", but the Bible tells us that we become the housing, the temple of Holy Spirit.

We are the place where the Spirit of God dwells. There was the ark of animals, the ark of the covenant, the temple itself, and Jesus could be considered an ark of God. We are the ark of Holy Spirit, the ark of God in the modern context, until Jesus shows up again.

This is why even the notion of Holy Spirit is a faith journey. I remember reading something that really shook me when I began to understand it. In John 16, Jesus is with His disciples and tells them something that seems unreal.

"But I am telling you the truth: it is better for you that I go away, because if I do not go, the Helper [Holy Spirit] will not come to you. But if I do go away, then I will send him to you." (John 16:7)

"It's better for you."

Are you crazy? What an insane statement Jesus makes. How could it be better? Other translations would say "it's to our advantage" or "more profitable" that Jesus leaves. Profitable. Because of Jesus, we receive the greatest exchange, our sins for freedom and life, and Jesus Himself says it's better and more profitable that He leaves. Why would He say this?

Because He's right.

Let's just think briefly about Holy Spirit's working in the Old Testament. People may think miracles don't happen in their lives until they have an experience with Holy Spirit baptism (again, more on that later). But the truth is when we look anywhere in the Bible before Acts 2, we will see miracles, signs, and wonders. In fact, some of the craziest ones to me are found in the Old Testament. The power is comparable to that of the New Testament but the quantity, or the availability, is so much greater. Jesus is addressing that Holy Spirit is not just for a select few but for everyone. His availability is better for humanity.

It's better without Jesus here. It's better because Jesus is no longer in one place at one time doing the work of the Father. Rather, Holy Spirit is able to be with and have relationship with each of us at once. Jesus is no longer confined to a body but is present as the body of Christ all over the world, since the same Spirit of Jesus is now in us and can be upon us.

Jesus isn't just saying it's good for Him to leave. He's

31

letting us know that it is only when He leaves that Holy Spirit will come, and it's better for Holy Spirit to come. Think about it: Jesus lived closely with twelve people. He spent a majority of His time with three of the twelve. Don't you want to be one of those three? Imagine this: Jesus shows up at your job that you hate, or even love, and He asks you to go on a journey that billions of people would dream about. There are billions of people who would do anything to take that offer. What Jesus is saying is that now we can and should. Jesus was limited to a body, but we have Holy Spirit, who is sent by God the Father and who isn't confined to one body. Anybody can have Holy Spirit with them wherever their body goes! We no longer have to get to Jesus, because Jesus decided it is better for us to have Holy Spirit—who gets to us, inside of us, and even upon us.

That verse, the moment in John 16 when Jesus says, "… it is better for you that I go away …", is the idea behind this book. The idea is that if we can understand the gravity behind those words that Jesus said Himself, we and the people around us will be empowered to lead completely different lives.

WHY JESUS SAYS IT'S BETTER

1. JESUS SAID SO

What I've experienced and the entire idea of this book come right from the mouth of Jesus. Jesus says that it's better for us, it's to our advantage, it's to our profit, that

He leaves and Holy Spirit comes. Jesus makes this His last statement ever while on earth. Immediately afterward, Jesus basically flies into the sky. He could have taught us to fly, but He instead chose to tell us about Holy Spirit. I want to put myself in the shoes or sandals or thongs (sandal joke) of the disciples and feel what they may have felt. I mean, come on. We're all with Jesus and He shows one of us how to walk on water, but then we find out He can basically fly. How upset would you be that He didn't teach that? So, Holy Spirit is better than flying.

The Bible doesn't share what they felt in that moment, but if it was me, I would be ticked. There's no other word … well, there is but, you know. I would be so upset because it doesn't really make sense. It doesn't make sense that it would be better for Him—the one I followed, experienced a new life with, saw performing miracles, saw die and be raised to life for me—to leave. How could it possibly be better that He leaves, and in His early 30s at that? It's better because Jesus said so. As the disciples soon find out, life really becomes better. They are filled with His power and do more than before.

2. YOU GET MORE FACETIME WITH JESUS THAN THE DISCIPLES HAD

When Jesus was on the earth, He often secluded Himself in order to spend time with the Father. But now that we have Holy Spirit with us, He never leaves our side. If anything, Holy Spirit is speaking to the Father on our behalf even when we're asleep. The disciples used to wake Jesus up. These days, Holy Spirit waits for us to wake up. How funny it must be to Jesus to go from having to be woken up when in a storm to Holy Spirit waking us up when we are in one.

I think about the story of the paralyzed man who gets carried by his four friends to Jesus. Can I be 100 percent honest? I barely have enough friends to drive me to the airport on a given day, let alone people who would carry me to another town. If I was in the group that was asked to carry someone to another city, I'd probably wait to see if the stronger guys spoke up first. Thank Jesus that we no longer have to carry our friends to another city, break into someone's house, and lower them to Jesus. That's a great story of faith, friendship, and the love of Jesus, but imagine that story today. You'd go to jail.

Most of us probably know of at least one friend or person in our lives who is sick. If you do, what would happen if you brought them to Jesus? We can bring people to Him by praying for them. I don't mean just reaching out and saying, "I'm praying for you." I mean actually asking, "Can I pray with you?" The difference between "I'm praying for you" and "Can I pray with you?" is often the same difference between a sick friend and a healed one. In my experience, I've seen God move when I've stepped out in faith and prayed for someone rather than when I simply say that I am praying. We need to understand that Jesus still heals the sick. He can do that through us, our hands and our prayer, with Holy Spirit empowering us. Of course, God doesn't need me in order to heal someone, but why not take part in what He's doing and go along for the ride?

Think of it like this. If you were sick and Jesus entered the room, would He heal you? Absolutely. We get to do that for others. We aren't Jesus, but the same Spirit lives in us.

3. IT BUILDS OUR FAITH

"Blessed are those who have not seen, and yet have believed." (John 20:29)

Jesus says that we are actually blessed because we believe without seeing Him. Since Jesus is no longer on the earth, and hasn't been for at least 2,000 plus years, our faith grows stronger with every generation who hasn't seen the face of Jesus but still believes that He is real.

We have an amazing opportunity to believe in what we cannot see, and that is an idea of what faith is. When you don't see the healing, when you don't see the provision, when you don't see the future, you can trust the one who is the healing, the provision, and the future—even if you haven't seen Him.

4. THE PRECEDENCE OF THE STATEMENT

Jesus is the best thing to ever walk on this earth, and Holy Spirit is the best thing to ever walk with us. Jesus did more than anyone has ever done alone. He says that greater things will be done but, clearly, Jesus isn't talking about greater miracles, because what could be better than raising the dead? I believe He means "greater in number." The same goes for His statement that Holy Spirit is better for us. "Us" is referring to humanity. We are better off because the Spirit of Jesus can be in everyone, not just those who are able to get to Him. There are no longer just 12 disciples. There are billions. Billions. Because Jesus left to send us Holy Spirit.

The moment that Jesus left, He gave us permission to receive what was next. What's next for you?

THE THRONE

How cool would it be to have a throne? Instead of coming home and sitting on the couch, wouldn't it be cool, even just once, to come home and sit on a throne? I mean, that would be pretty odd and would take up a ton of space, and we don't really do that in our culture anymore. But thrones are a very real thing in heaven. The idea of the throne helps us see where things are in time.

First and foremost, God is on the throne as you read this. The throne is not on Earth, which Jesus tells us when He teaches us how to pray: "Our Father who is in heaven …" (Matthew 6:9). This helps us understand that God is in heaven and we are not. We aren't on the throne, and it's for the best. I love that narrative in the Bible when the mother comes to Jesus and asks that each of her sons sit by Him. I think that's the most mom thing ever, right? That would be equivalent to when moms tell the little league coach to make their kid the team captain. It's really all a big joke because it doesn't change anything, but it's still cute that it matters. Not only is God on the throne, but He's been there for a hot minute. Technically, He's outside of time and space, so there's no way to really know how long. But it's been a long time. Forever, really.

Right next to Him is Jesus.

Jesus is at the right hand of the Father, which would again be problematic for the mom who wants her sons on each side of Jesus, but whatever. Jesus deserves the seat on the throne, and I would never want to be on it. I can't imagine the weight of that. Jesus is on the throne after doing His 33-year sentence on the earth. If you think of His time here in comparison to being with the Father, it's like a jail sentence, which makes it that much more powerful that Jesus would do it. And let's not forget how He came into the picture.

Jesus' last words were about waiting for a gift. Gifts are always worth waiting for. Gifts we receive from others are free (for us) and have our names on them. The same is true about Holy Spirit. Holy Spirit is Jesus' gift to humanity, so we can have the same relationship the disciples had and even greater.

IT DOESN'T END WITH JESUS

Maybe it's just me, but the word "candor" always sounds like the name of a planet from a sci-fi movie. But I want to have complete candor that I know saying "it doesn't end with Jesus" may seem strange. Let me be candor, or have candor, or whatever the phrase is …

Jesus isn't the end of our story. Jesus isn't the destination. He isn't even the goal. How can I say that? Well, Jesus did Himself.

When Jesus mentioned His goal, which wasn't just to free Israel like the people wanted, He was creating a way for people to get to God the Father.

I don't think enough people understand how amazing God the Father is. How have we made Christianity all about Jesus when Jesus made it all about the Father? Jesus would say that He only does what He sees the Father doing. He even asks the Father permission to do things and spends a lot of time with Him. Holy Spirit leads us to Jesus and then empowers us to live more like Jesus, who is getting us to the Father.

THE FATHER ISSUE

Why have we put Holy Spirit in second place? One of the reasons is because the generations before us have traditionally had bad fathers. I'm not saying you didn't have a good dad, but there is a monumental difference between a dad and a father.

Side note: When people pray out loud and say, "Daddy God …", it's just freaking weird. Please stop. Let me be your friend and let you know you're making everyone uncomfortable.

I truly believe that the level of strife we may have in our relationship with our earthly father correlates to our viewpoint of the heavenly One. It makes sense, doesn't it? The only father you can really relate to is the one you're born with. Of course, many of us have father figures who instill things in us our dads never did, and that helps bridge the gap. I have heard it said that your relationship with God mirrors the one you have with your father; your relationship with Jesus mirrors the ones you have with your friends; and your relationship with Holy Spirit mirrors the one you have with your mother. It's an interesting idea, for sure. In many regards, I do think that it's true.

I have even gotten into a habit of thinking through what I feel my relationship with Jesus, God the Father, and God the Holy Spirit look like. I have found I pray differently based on what part of the Godhead I think about. When you pray for a word, I would encourage you to think of what God would give you, what Jesus would give you, and what Holy Spirit would give you. You may find that you hear different things.

JESUS IS THE WAY

Here's something that I have been thinking and praying about for a while now: Jesus isn't the destination. Jesus is the bridge. "No one comes to the Father except through me ..." (John 14:6) In a moment of fear, Thomas, one of Jesus' disciples, asks where Jesus is going. Jesus comforts Thomas with His answer, letting him know that He is the bridge to the Father.

Jesus is the bridge—not the destination. Jesus is the way and not the end. Jesus makes a way for us to go on the journey. Holy Spirit walks with us on that journey, and we get to be with the Father when we are in heaven.

Have we made the starting line the finish line? When we got close to Jesus and received the salvation He has for us, did we unintentionally end the journey to relationship with God the Father? I think these are healthy questions to ask ourselves from time to time.

I think we can wrap up this whole idea with this: God the Father is amazing. God the Son, Jesus, is amazing. God the Holy Spirit is amazing, as well. We need the fullness of God, not just Jesus, not just God the Father, and not just Holy Spirit. We should pursue all that God has for us and all of who God is.

BETTER THAN JESUS

Holy Spirit is the best thing since sliced bread and Jesus. Jesus wants us to have Holy Spirit so much that He left the very earth He created, His friends and family, and all those who needed Him. He left us to leave us something of greater impact. This is really the whole idea that what Jesus did, we can now participate in.

The only thing better than Jesus with us is Jesus within us.

Holy Spirit is God within us.

REFLECTIONS

What phrase is more impactful to you: "It is finished," or "But you will receive power..."

_____

_____

_____

_____

_____

What do you feel Holy Spirit speaking to you in this chapter?

_____

_____

_____

_____

Would you rather have Jesus with you or have Jesus within you?

_____

_____

_____

_____

_____

BETTER THAN JESUS

More Than Salvation

The thought of having something better than Jesus is tied to also having more than salvation. Salvation is great, but it's just the start. No one goes to the Olympics to see the start of the race. They go to see who finishes and the subsequent journey to that point; the start is the minimum expectation.

I have been saved so many times in my life that it's ridiculous. I've been told that when I was four years old, I prayed that special prayer (which, clearly, wasn't even all that special since I'm not even certain if I was four or not). When I was a little older, I was on a plane that had to have an emergency landing, and I must have gotten saved at least 20 times in just a matter of minutes. In middle school, things got a little more real for me. During winter of my sixth-grade year, I went to a church camp in the upper peninsula of Michigan. It was so cold that I had to walk across a frozen lake to get to the chapel each night. I remember it so well, because I wore a layer of gym shorts, a winter coat, and boots to keep me warm. That weekend, I got serious about giving my whole life to Jesus. I accepted what He had done for me on the cross and through resurrection; I was truly born again. I also had an encounter with Holy Spirit that weekend.

I remember praying at the altar late on a particular night, as our camp days were usually pretty long. We'd prayed for multiple things, which I can't recall now. One thing I remember is having to do an activity with a name tag. We were all given name tags where we were supposed to write a new identity. I know I didn't fully understand what was happening, because I just wrote the name Jeff. Clearly missed that moment.

There was another moment I didn't miss out on and that was prayer for baptism in the Holy Spirit. I went to the altar and as I was being prayed over, I didn't feel any differently. But I know one thing for sure—I spoke a language that wasn't English (more on that in a little bit).

A couple of days later, I was getting off of the school bus to walk inside Jefferson Middle School in Midland, Michigan, when I remembered praying for the Holy Spirit at camp. Instantly, my faith increased. So, what did I do next? I did my best sprint from the sidewalk to the grass in front of the brick-covered school building. I was convinced that the Holy Spirit had made me faster as a spiritual gift. At the time, I was really into reading comics, so I think there may have been a slight correlation.

There are a couple of problems with this. First, I was not fast. In fact, I was going through a phase, and I'm not just talking about puberty. I was chubby. I lived right behind a doughnut shop and would ride my bike one block to buy one. In my mind, the bike ride counted against the doughnut, or three, I would eat. I was a very chubby sixth grader and, to be fully honest, I wasn't super aware of it. I wore a lot of funny T-shirts, like one that read, "I can only please one person a day. Today is not your day. Tomorrow's not looking so good either." The worst, though, (which shows how out of touch I was with how large I was) was a shirt that read, "I'm in shape. Round is a shape." Maybe that's funny if you're a dad and you've gained a couple pounds, but I was at a place in my life when I was starting to look like I would need a seatbelt extender somewhere down the line. I eventually left that part of my life … at least, I think I did?

So, you have a zealous, chubby sixth-grade boy who believes God has given him speed ability—which doesn't end well, as I'm sure you can imagine. This went on for about a week until I challenged one of my friends who didn't love Jesus to a race. I think somewhere in my head I thought that if I could use my super speed and beat the unsaved kid, then he would have no other option but to declare Jesus as Lord of his life. I didn't win the race. He

47

didn't give his life to Jesus. I'm pretty sure he's actually in jail for drug dealing. So … he could outrun me but not the police?

As funny as this is, I really had no idea what it looked like to have more of Jesus in my life. I had salvation down to a science because I was asking for it about every 20 minutes. Salvation has one of the most interesting phrases attached to it, specifically because we almost always use the word "saved" in the past tense. We so often say, "I got saved when I was this-many-years old…" or "Have you gotten saved?" The problem is that so many people try to get salvation and keep it. Salvation is not something you get or attain; salvation is a change to who you are. Once you give your life to Jesus, it's not the end. It's the start.

I spent most of my childhood and teenage years just trying to survive salvation. I felt like I was losing that thing as much as I lose my keys now. Every single time I sinned, I would feel as if God had left me or broken up with me. For the record, you don't have to feel this way. Of course, some of those emotions probably come from childhood experience of divorce and parents' involvement in multiple breakups, but the problem is that most people live like this. They live life with Jesus, always afraid that He is going to leave.

There is a difference between salvation and sanctification. Salvation is what God does for us in a moment of our choosing Him. After that, sanctification is ongoing within us with every choice we make.

SIN

Can we pause and talk about sin for a moment? It'll be quick. I promise.

There is no place in the Bible that says that you have to sin after you are born again.

A great question to ask ourselves is, "Am I just trying to religiously live out salvation, or have I actually been born again? Am I a new creation, or am I still the old but trying to work out my religious duties?" We are called by God to die to our old selves and become new. When your old self dies, your old self's actions should follow. Will it take some time? Yes, but the goal is to get closer to our heavenly Father on a daily basis. Your old habits will have to die off. That's another reason to be in a community of people who have been there before. The hope is we will quit sinning cold turkey, but the truth for some of us is that our old habits are a part of us. Luckily, we just need to kill that part and let it die off.

Weirdly enough, I feel as if people joke about how they still sin or how it's impossible to stop sinning. The excuse is usually, "Well, we all mess up," or "We are all born to sin." The truth is: We are born into the nature of sin, but when we are born again, when we give our lives to what Jesus did for us on the cross, we die to that sinful nature. If you have given your life to Jesus and still have a problem with sin, it's either because you haven't really died to yourself, you haven't gotten help with being sanctified, or you are choosing to sin. Sin is often a choice. You are no longer your nature; you are what you nurture. This is why it's so key to not do this faith journey with just you and Jesus. You and Jesus are enough to change the world, but we all need community and counsel to be changed into who Jesus wants us to be. I'm reminded of all the times I've had blind spots to even what Jesus might be screaming at me. I have people in my life who can notice my blind spots and help me hear what Holy Spirit is trying to tell me, things I may not hear in my lonely solace.

THERE IS MORE

If life was all about getting our sins forgiven, then wouldn't it make sense that we would immediately disappear and be sent to heaven to hang out with God once we give our lives to Jesus? Why would Jesus keep hanging around after He rises from the dead? Why would He tell His disciples to go and make disciples? Why would He tell us to go and wait to receive more?

Jesus sets up this idea of getting more than salvation the moment He steps onto the scene. Technically, it would have taken a while because He was a baby and would have to learn to walk, but you get the point. Jesus shows us that there is more than just "being saved." He shows us through the Great Commission and who He sends after He leaves the earth.

BAPTISM IN THE HOLY SPIRIT

If you currently aren't baptized in Holy Spirit, that doesn't make you any less than those who have been, or any less loved by God. If anyone has told you that you don't have enough or that it's not your time yet, they are an idiot and they have no idea what they are talking about.

When we are born again, Holy Spirit comes to live inside of us. When we are baptized in the Holy Spirit, He comes upon us (Acts 1:8). Imagine an empty glass, representing who we are before being born again. We are empty. Now imagine a glass filled to the top. This represents who we are when we are born again and Holy Spirit is within us. If a hose was pouring water into the glass so that the water flows over and upon the cup, that's what baptism in the Holy Spirit is like. Baptism means "to be fully submerged." Baptism in the Holy Spirit is our constant submersion in Holy Spirit. Another way to think of salvation is Holy Spirit in us, while baptism in the Holy Spirit is us in Holy Spirit. There is an indwelling then an outpouring due to an overflow of Holy Spirit's power and love in our lives.

In the passage below, you're going to read the words "Spirit of God." That's Holy Spirit—same person just different vernacular. My legal name is Tyler, but everyone calls me Ty—same person just a different way of addressing me. We see this in Genesis 1:2 and other passages of Scripture, as well.

*And when Jesus was baptized, immediately he went up from the water, and behold, the heavens were opened to him, and he saw the **Spirit of God** descending like a dove and **coming to rest upon Him**; and behold, a voice from heaven said, "This is my beloved Son, with whom I am well pleased." (Matthew 3:16-17)*

A fascinating thing is that there are no recorded miracles in the Bible until after Holy Spirit comes upon Jesus. Did Jesus do miracles before then? There are a number of reasons why there is a very good possibility that He did, but I find it interesting that none are recorded until He is baptized in the Holy Spirit. Afterward, there is an immediate increase in the amount and constancy of miracles that take place. This is how it should be for us. Jesus' ministry really begins at this point, and our greater effectiveness begins at the same point. After Holy Spirit comes upon us, we will experience more than we did before.

MORE THAN BEFORE

A more straightforward way of thinking about Holy Spirit baptism is that it is more than before. In the simplest terms, that's the truth of it. It's more than what we receive at salvation. It's more than salvation. It's the empowerment to bring others into what we've experienced. Jesus wants us to have this.

On one occasion, while he was eating with them, he gave them this command: "Do not leave Jerusalem, but wait for the gift my Father promised, which you have heard me speak about. For John baptized with water, but in a few days you will be baptized with the Holy Spirit." (Acts 1:4-5)

Jesus is telling the disciples what they are to do after He leaves. We should also follow Jesus' command to be baptized in the Holy Spirit. What's amazing is that anyone who has received Jesus can have this gift.

"But you will receive power when the Holy Spirit has come upon you, and you will be my witnesses in Jerusalem and in all Judea and Samaria, and to the end of the earth." (Acts 1:8)

Jesus goes beyond saying they should receive the gift of Holy Spirit. He begins explaining what that entails. We will receive power when Holy Spirit is not only within us but comes upon us. He will then empower us to be greater witnesses of Jesus everywhere. When I was a kid, the idea of "witnessing" was almost like a verb that you do to other people, but it's actually not that at all. We are empowered to be witnesses of Jesus' image, meaning that we don't witness to others, but others should see Jesus when they witness us. There is only one issue here: If you aren't already being a witness for Jesus, there's nothing to empower. Holy Spirit will empower you to be a greater witness, but you need to actually live a life that looks like, or pursues looking like, Jesus. We have the gift, command, and empowerment of Holy Spirit in order for us to see the same things Jesus saw, so that other people see those things, too. When they do, they'll see Jesus.

When the day of Pentecost arrived, they were all together in one place. And suddenly there came from heaven a sound like a mighty rushing wind, and it filled the entire house where they were sitting. And divided tongues as of fire appeared to them and rested on each one of them. **And they were all filled with the Holy Spirit** *and began to speak in other tongues as the Spirit gave them utterance. (Acts 2:1-4)*

Many times, we try to subtract ourselves from more. We can end up disqualifying ourselves due to our insecurity, but this is not the place to do that. In Acts 1, Jesus calls baptism in the Holy Spirit a gift, and it's a gift with your name on it. You would have to be crazy to deny a gift with your name on it from God Himself! I so love that the first time people are baptized in the Holy Spirit, everyone who is seeking receives it. The Bible says they were all filled with the Holy Spirit and began to speak in other tongues. It gets even better. Right after this, the people who are empowered to share about Jesus with more power and authority (this doesn't mean they start yelling or shouting at people; it means they're more loving beyond their means) end up telling others what has happened to them. Thousands of people turn their lives toward Jesus. Thousands.

That can be you. You can see thousands of people come to Jesus. Not by yourself—but with Holy Spirit.

HOW TO RECEIVE THIS

You can receive baptism in the Holy Spirit anywhere. (Okay, maybe not in line at the DMV because that's basically hell, but everywhere else is probably solid.) If you want to receive this empowerment, it's really simple. Get to a place where you can get close to Holy Spirit. This might be a prayer closet, your living room, your car, or even your bathroom where you get ready in the mornings. Start the conversation with Jesus, since He is the baptizer, and let Him know that you want this gift. Tell Him in your own words, and keep praying. Just like you would receive a gift with your name on it on your birthday or Christmas, receive it. Calm your thoughts and allow Holy Spirit to move in and through you. At any point you gain faith, feeling, or the knowledge that Holy Spirit is with you, receive the gift and speak out whatever you feel Him prompting you to say. This is speaking in tongues.

On another note, right now is a great time to pause and pray to receive this. Get into a place and mindset where you have already been able to hear from or receive something from God before. Remember, Jesus called this a gift, and this one has your name on it. You don't beg for gifts with your name on it. Let Jesus know you want to receive all that He has for you. Keep praying and let Holy Spirit come upon you. When you know Holy Spirit is with you and He feels closer than usual, speak out anything you feel Him prompting you to say. It won't make any sense to you, and that's normal. It's a new language. How would it make any sense to you if you've never

55

spoken it before? You got this.

A NOTE TO THOSE WHO HAVE ALREADY EXPERIENCED THIS

If you haven't yet experienced baptism in the Holy Spirit, you can skip this section because I'm about to take some people to church.

Friend, if you have received baptism in the Holy Spirit, which is the empowerment to lead people to Jesus, and you aren't leading people to Jesus, you need to get over yourself. You've been empowered with something that people in the Old Testament would kill for. If it's been a long time since you've loved someone into relationship with Jesus, you need to love better and share more. I'm not saying to get on a box at Walmart and preach a message, but your life should be a reflection of the life of Jesus. People should be so attracted to what you have that they ask you about it. Even if they don't ask, you've been empowered to offer that love to them.

"But I get nervous telling others about Jesus." Get over yourself. Put away your ego and pride, and share the eternal gift you've received that is Jesus Christ. You've been empowered to steal people from hell. It's not your pastor's job. It's your job to get your friends and family to Jesus. So, please do it.

Don't make excuses; make disciples. (For the record, it's kind of the Great Commission.)

REFLECTIONS

What excites you the most about the idea that Jesus had more for us than salvation?

_____

What should change in your life when you're baptized in the Holy Spirit?

_____

If you have already received more than salvation, have people around you been impacted by that?

_____

BETTER THAN JESUS

Can I Get A Copy Of My Receipt

When Holy Spirit is brought up in conversation, church, or at any time, really, it seems there is one thing people love to talk about more than others: speaking in tongues.

I would like to be the first to say that speaking in tongues is the weirdest thing in the Bible to me. I talk about this for a living, and it's still weird to me. So, just be aware that we're in the same boat. Let's be honest, if you don't understand what speaking in tongues is really for, the benefit and why we can access it, then it's weird. It's a little weird even when you do understand all of that. Suddenly, we are able to speak a language that we don't know. It's either really weird, or it's the closest thing to being in a comic book.

BETTER THAN JESUS

I think we can almost tend to believe that speaking in tongues was an accident in Holy Spirit's lab. When we really understand what it is and what it does for us, it can become the greatest tool for our spiritual journey.

WHAT IS YOUR FAVORITE FRUIT?

Let's say you invite me to a party you're throwing and ask me to bring one thing—bananas, your favorite fruit. As I'm on the way to your party, I head to the grocery store to buy a bunch of bananas. I arrive at your party and people are having a great time. You see me and are so excited because you know I've brought some bananas. (I don't know what kind of party this is, but stay with me.) But you don't see me carrying any bananas and you get disappointed, which totally makes sense. You ask me where the bananas are and I tell you that I do, in fact, have the bananas. Your eyes light up. You look around once more and begin to get excited with expectation.

I pull a receipt out of my pocket, and wouldn't you know it? The receipt says that I bought a bunch of bananas. You are thrilled. I came through and didn't let you down. Of course, you then ask me for the bananas. I hand you the receipt. You look at me puzzled but thank me, nonetheless. Once you're holding the receipt that states bananas were purchased, again, you ask me where the bananas are. I tell you that the receipt says I got them, so you don't need anything else. You walk away confused and disappointed.

Speaking in tongues is the receipt for the heavenly transaction of being baptized in the Holy Spirit.

Yet so many have made the receipt the goal when it isn't. If we make baptism in the Holy Spirit all about speaking in tongues, we will end up being discouraged in the long run. Every time I have spoken and prayed for people to receive Spirit baptism, there has always been someone who was once told that speaking in tongues is the goal or the mark of spiritual maturity. The goal of the receipt is to let us know we have been baptized in the Holy Spirit, along with some amazing side benefits.

If you have been baptized in the Holy Spirit and speak in tongues but you haven't led someone to be born again, then you need to check yourself. Remember, one of the main reasons Jesus tells His disciples to receive this gift is so they can be empowered as witnesses for Him. The fact that we are able to speak in tongues as well as have the intimacy it creates are amazing bonuses. We need to be leading people to Jesus both in prayer and in love.

You don't have to pray for someone in order for them to be touched by Jesus through you. You might give an extra-large tip, buy someone's groceries, or call up that person who is rude to you on a regular basis just to love on them. Many of us found Jesus because someone who already had Jesus led us to Him. Now, it's your turn.

WHY SHOULD WE SPEAK IN TONGUES?

BETTER THAN JESUS

I don't know if you can relate to this, but there are many days when my prayers seem to go on for three or four hours. I'm praying so much that I know I've lost track of time. Then I look at the clock and realize only seven minutes have passed. Have you ever been there? I feel like this happens to me on a weekly basis. In my mind, I've already solved all the world's problems, and it seems as if there is nothing else I could possibly pray, only to find out I've been praying for just a few moments. To be clear, while both are beneficial, I think quality time with Holy Spirit is far better than quantity time.

1. PRAY GOD'S WILL

What if I told you that instead of having to figure out what to pray, God could tell you what to pray? When we pray in tongues or in the Spirit (which is the same thing, just a different vernacular), we end up praying the perfect will of God and He prays through us. This coincides with what Jesus tells us about to how to pray. *"Our Father who is in heaven, hallowed be your name. Your kingdom come, your will be done ..."* God's will, not ours. We aren't asking God to step in and write a blank check. We are asking Him to let us into His plan for us.

Jesus tells us to pray for God's will, but when we pray in tongues, we aren't praying for God's will. Rather, we're praying God's actual will. We go from positioning ourselves to receive to mobilizing and receiving at the same time.

In the same way, the Spirit helps us in our weakness. We do not know what we ought to pray for, but the Spirit himself intercedes for us through wordless groans. (Romans 8:26)

2. GROW YOUR FAITH

I really believe that one of the most, if not the most, faithful things you can do is pray in tongues. Think about the fact that you are praying God's will for you, which is amazing, and you don't know what you're praying. You can let your imagination and faith run wild pontificating what you're praying when you pray in tongues. I was 12 years old when I was baptized in the Holy Spirit and began to speak in tongues. I could've been praying the address of my first home, my wife's name, or the dreams that would one day become reality. I can't wait to stand before God the Father and ask Him how many times He answered prayers that I didn't even know I'd prayed.

*But you, dear friends, **by building yourselves up in your most holy faith and praying in the Holy Spirit**, keep yourselves in God's love as you wait for the mercy of our Lord Jesus Christ to bring you to eternal life. (Jude 1:20-21)*

*For if you have the ability to speak in tongues, you will be talking only to God, since people won't be able to understand you. You will be speaking by the power of the Spirit, but **it will all be mysterious.** (1 Corinthians 14:2)*

1 Corinthians 14:2 says that everything spoken in tongues will all be mysterious, and that's where faith is

activated. You are praying God's perfect will through you, for you, and for others who you don't even know yet. In many ways, you are being prophetic. If you're in a rough situation in your life, you could always think, "What if I have already prayed myself through this situation?" When we pray in tongues, I believe we step into God's timeline.

On the other side of this, we may also experience times when it seems like God isn't answering or hearing our prayers at all. Could it be that when a prayer goes unanswered, it's because God has a better prayer for you to pray? I don't want us going down a rabbit trail of thinking of the right thing to pray, because I believe we should pray about what we want to pray, not what we think we should pray. Take out the religion and add the real relationship. It's way more fun and healthier, too.

FAQ 1: DOES HOLY SPIRIT MOVE MY MOUTH?

Let's get into why speaking in tongues is amazing. There are a bunch of benefits to praying in tongues. First is that it's evidence of having Holy Spirit not just within us but upon us. The best indicator that we have been baptized in the Holy Spirit is that we begin to speak in tongues.

Let's pause. Holy Spirit doesn't make us do anything. We are free to speak or not speak. We can be loud (no, thanks) or quiet when we do so. Holy Spirit isn't literally moving our mouths or tongues around. That would be terrifying. We are in full control of when and how we speak what Holy Spirit prompts us to speak. This isn't something we make up, like:

"She came in a Honda and left in a Kia."

"Shoulda bought a Honda."

(If you say those out loud, you'll get the joke.)

FAQ 2: WHO CAN SPEAK IN TONGUES?

If you're asking, then you can. Once you are born again, having allowed Jesus into your life, you are a candidate for this gift. Remember that this is a gift (Acts 1:4), and this gift has your name on it. You don't have to beg for what God wants to give you. You just have to receive it. You will begin to speak in tongues when you are baptized in the Holy Spirit, and it's going to be amazing.

FAQ 3: HOW OFTEN SHOULD I PRAY IN TONGUES?

You should pray in tongues as much as you want to step into God's prayer for you, and as much as you want to grow in faith. For me, there is no ratio or "prayer plan." I just pray in English as long as I have words to say. When I don't know what to pray, or when I want more prayer over a situation, I pray in tongues. Again, I don't pray what I think I should pray. I pray about what I want to pray about. I think of prayer as talking to God, because that's what it really is. Prayer is a conversation with the divine, and praying in tongues is a divine conversation.

BETTER THAN JESUS

You just do you. Don't overthink it.

REFLECTIONS

If you could pray what God wanted, would you pray more or less?

_____

_____

_____

_____

_____

What does your prayer life look like right now?

_____

_____

_____

_____

_____

How can you battle the thoughts and feeligns or not praying good enough or long enough?

_____

_____

_____

_____

_____

67

BETTER THAN JESUS

Holy Spirit In Us

"Giving your life to Jesus" sounds like a pretty bizarre statement in itself. Giving your life to Jesus isn't a past tense event but a choice you make every day. When you give your life to Jesus, you give Him your past so He can forgive you. Then you give Him your current state so you can move forward toward a future in heaven with the Father. Giving your life to Jesus is determined at the end of it.

This is where the journey of better than Jesus really begins. In no way am I saying to make Jesus past tense, but Jesus wants us to have Holy Spirit. He wants us to be empowered to do more than just not sin. We don't hang out with people just because they don't murder us. We hang out with people because it's better than being by ourselves, and we get to be with people we enjoy and who make us better.

The Bible is pretty clear that once we confess Jesus as Lord of our lives, accept what He did for us on the cross, and repent of our sins, we will have Holy Spirit within us. In a way, we are inviting Holy Spirit into our lives. The Bible mentions that we become the temple, or the housing, of Holy Spirit (1 Corinthians 6), which implies that He's within us wherever we go. It is so exciting that I can wake up every morning and Holy Spirit is right there with me, ready for the day! We are there for the adventure of what He has for us, not the other way around.

LET HIM IN

The Holy Spirit is active even before we invite Him into our lives. He knocks at the door of our hearts (some would call that conviction). The first moment you ever had with Holy Spirit was, most likely, a convicting or convincing one. Whether you realized something about God, or you had a moment that could only happen because of God, Holy Spirit was a part of it, as He is God on Earth. We invite Holy Spirit into our lives on a regular basis. Every morning, I try my best to dedicate my day to Holy Spirit, to get in step with Him, whether while getting ready or while driving. The truth is, sometimes I don't get around to it, but I still get to invite Him into my everyday choices. What's so great about having Holy Spirit in us, cultivating relationship with us, is that we can invite Him into more than just our generic day.

We can invite Him into everything, because He is with us wherever we go.

Most people I know who have some level of relationship with God do something that I wouldn't necessarily say is bad, but there is something better. How they consult Holy Spirit when making choices, whether big or small, is somewhat odd. I see this so often, and I used to do it in the earlier days of my faith journey. I would have a choice to make, and I would pray about it. What I mean is that I would tell God my options then passively tell Him which one He should tell me to pick. You can judge me, but you do it all the time. It goes a little like this:

"Dear God, (I don't know why we say that, as if we are writing a letter to Him or something) I have these two options before me and I need Your help (even though we don't most of the time—we just want to feel spiritual about the choice we've, basically, already made). The first option doesn't feel right, so I'm already done talking about it. Now, let me tell You about option number two. This has Your name written all over it. I'm going to choose option two. Would You bless my decision? Amen."

I would pray this way all the time. I was checking the box, acting like I was inviting God in. In a way, I was, but I was inviting Him into what I was already planning to do. I was asking for spiritual insurance for my choice. I often, we often, end up begging God for what we want to happen.

These prayers aren't bad, but there's something better.

What if, instead of asking God to bless our decisions, we heard from Holy Spirit, who lives within us for these exact moments, to direct our paths and show us what to do? I don't always hear an answer, and there will be times when you don't, either. But that shouldn't paralyze us in our decisions. It just means we make the decision without that extra nudge in the right direction, which isn't inherently bad. If anything, we grow the most in making healthy biblical decisions when we feel like He isn't speaking. Those are the decisions that change us and our future. They move us from always needing to hear God's voice to knowing His voice even when we don't hear it because we've heard it before.

We can hear from Holy Spirit in more than just prayer. We can hear from Him through reading the pages of the Word of God, as well. However, I don't want us to get stuck because we haven't felt a push or pull from Holy Spirit to do something. If you have the Word of God and Jesus, you'll be okay.

What is so amazing is that when we hear Holy Spirit's voice regarding a choice we are going to make, we don't have to ask God to bless that choice. If it's God's choice, it's already blessed.

These are the moments that build our character. The Holy Spirit in us builds our character and produces amazing fruit in our lives.

Let us allow Holy Spirit into our lives in a deeper way than ever before. When we invite Him into the deepest parts of us, spiritual substance and growth should occur. Fruit should be produced. The Bible calls this "fruit of the Holy Spirit"—fruit that is produced when the Holy Spirit is around us.

When something is produced in us, it is created, or grown, over time. When we have Holy Spirit within is, we should continually develop His fruit.

FRUIT

Before we talk about the fruit that is produced, I want to share how we get it, since it's no good to be hungry for something if there's no way to get to what we are hungry for. There is one very simple rule for how we obtain the fruit of Holy Spirit: hang out with the one who has the fruit. By name, it's the fruit of Holy Spirit; therefore, it's of Him, just like this book is the book of Ty Buckingham. (I wouldn't really say it like that, but it's true.) The more we hang out with Holy Spirit, the more the fruit grows within us. There are nine fruits of Holy Spirit, and they don't come naturally to us, unless we create an environment where it becomes natural for them to grow.

The first way to get them to grow is by hanging out with Holy Spirit. Another way is by hanging out with people who have already produced the fruit.

I have never been good at growing things. When I was in elementary school, my mom took me to a home improvement store to get something, and I saw a section of seeds for sale. I was so excited! All of a sudden, I felt like I was being called to be a gardener. There was one particular seed that stood out to me: cactus. I bought the seed packets from the store (meaning my mom bought them), and I began the process of becoming a gardener. I got home, went to the backyard, and dug small holes to plant the seeds. I covered them up and stared at the place where I planted the cacti, somewhat expecting them to instantly jump out of the ground. I checked on my cacti every day, waiting for the yard to look like the outside of my grandparents' retirement home in Arizona. No luck. For days, weeks and months, there was no growth. To this day, those seeds are somewhere in the ground and haven't produced anything. And you know why? Because of the biggest part of the story that I've left out until now: I planted cactus seeds in Michigan in December—the wrong environment and the wrong season. I was doomed from the start.

SEASONS AND SECONDS

It was obviously silly, even as a small kid, to think that a cactus would instantly grow. Yet we think the same way about the fruit of Holy Spirit. We act like if we just pray, they'll grow, but that's not how it works. Farmers don't grow fruit out of the ground; they sow seed into it and let the earth do what it does best.

74

Fruit grows in seasons. One of my favorite things to hear people pray is, "God, give me patience. Right now. I pray for patience now." Do you see the humor? The idea of praying for any of the fruit to just appear is as silly as a farmer going out to a field, planting a seed, and waiting for it to grow overnight. You don't often see the fruit for a while. When you want the fruit of Holy Spirit, they start as seeds of faith, then grow roots that get deeper and stronger over time. By the time you actually see the fruit, there isn't usually only one fruit but many. You wouldn't plant an apple tree just for the first apple then cut it down, would you? Of course not. You'd plant that tree to give you sustained fruit over many seasons.

We grow the fruit of Holy Spirit through the seasons of our lives. We typically grow the fruit that we need the most in a particular season. The most time-sensitive seasons, when we want things right now, are usually when we develop patience. Be okay with the season you are in, because it may be the most fruitful season of your life.

LOW-HANGING FRUIT

The fruit of Holy Spirit are low-hanging fruit. When we begin understanding and letting Holy Spirit into our lives more, we start to grow deeper roots in Him. I recall learning that the fruit of Holy Spirit are not so much side effects of Holy Spirit in us but that they are fruit we're just supposed to have. It almost aligned with the ten commandments; it felt like another to-do list. But the fruit of Holy Spirit really are just that—fruit. They are the fruit produced when we allow Holy Spirit into our lives in a deeper sense than before. We control how much, or how little, fruit comes from our lives.

There are nine of these fruits listed in the Bible, but I don't find them to make up the exhaustive list of all the fruit of Holy Spirit. These are the pillars for where to start and stay in step with Holy Spirit. For example, there is actual fruit, like apples and bananas, which are popular fruits we all learn about as kids. There are others, like dragon-fruit (coolest name), which is most certainly a fruit, that may not be as well-known to some. In the same way, I think of grace, which naturally becomes a normal part of a believer's fruit basket, even though it's not listed as one of the nine fruits of Holy Spirit.

For too long, we've treated the fruit of Holy Spirit as if they are for children's church and cheesy Christian movies (don't get me started). The reality is that the fruit are what really make us believers. When we have Holy Spirit in us, a regeneration takes place, and our character and fruit develop.

LOVE

This is the foundation for all the other fruit. If you're not loving, all the other fruit go rotten. The fastest way to lose your fruit is to not love. Imagine you have all the peace in the world. If you aren't loving to those around you, that peace won't linger.

Generally speaking, we see love as an arbitrary feeling or moment when you like someone or something more than any of the others. Oftentimes, this love is based on comparison. What do you really love? Your mom, your spouse (I hope), maybe movies, or that new Thai restaurant that just opened up ... Why do we love these things? Because of how they make us feel and the experiences we have with them. Human love is based on self, but Holy Spirit is about loving others.

When I first met my wife, I didn't love her, because I didn't know her. As I got to know her, I loved her. I wanted to be around her because of how she made me feel when I walked into the room. Over a couple of weeks, I experienced a shift from wanting to be around her to trying to show her I'm good to be around, as well.

I do not believe in love at first sight, because love isn't something you feel or see; it's something you choose. Over time, you either choose to keep loving and growing in that love, or you begin to resent the very thing you used to love. Overall, the question is, are the fruits of the Holy Spirit about who we are or what we do? I believe it can be both. When I am loving, it determines my life. When I'm not loving, it deteriorates my life and the lives of those around me.

JOY

I've always heard people talk about joy, and it is regularly described in contrast to happiness. Often, it's said that happiness is situational, but joy is constant. Can we be real? When I go to my favorite restaurant near my house when it's supposed to be open, but it's closed, I feel no joy whatsoever. You may ask, "Well, isn't Jesus with you?" Clearly not. Otherwise, the restaurant would've been open. I'm joking, but joy seems to have the highest amount of pressure attached to it, as if you must have joy no matter what happens. Joy is a choice. Joy is a choice we get to make in every situation regardless of our feelings. Joy doesn't just happen. When you grow and mature, you make joy happen so that you have it even when you don't feel joyful. It's about looking toward the future and faithfully seeing that joy is coming, so you can choose to have it even now.

The joy of the Lord is my strength, but the joy of Ty is my weakness. I have found that what makes me joyful might not always be what makes Jesus joyful. I'm not talking about sin. I get joyful eating cheesecake, but it might kill me if that's all I do, whereas Holy Spirit has something amazing for me that produces joy, and maybe that is cheesecake from time to time (who knows?). My joy, what pumps me up, is all over the map. Again, I'm talking about joy, not happiness. Happiness is going to a movie. Joy is going to a movie with people who I love. The determining factor for my joy is whether something would make Jesus happy, not just me.

I don't see joy as being happy or as a feeling but as a fruit that is grown through hardship. The more difficult a situation, the sweeter the fruit of joy tastes. Have you been there? When you have a terrible day but stumble upon your favorite show, you see your best friend, or even a distant family member, the bad day suddenly fades away. Why? Because joy is contagious and will push emotions to the side. My wife and I have had some of the most joy in our marriage while going through the most difficult external circumstances. When you let your external become your internal, you haven't been intentional.

When you notice the good Holy Spirit does even amongst the bad in your life, even in hardship, you can have joy.

PEACE

Peace is knowing the unknown. Are you a peace-taker or a peacemaker? Are you waiting for things to get better, or are you spiritually hustling in the waiting? The best time to grow in peace is when things are crazy. Actually, you probably only grow in peace when you don't have it. You tend to grow in areas you don't have when you need to have them.

Holy Spirit's peace pairs perfectly with one of the names on His calling card: Comforter. To understand Holy Spirit peace is to understand Him as Comforter. We understand Him as Comforter when we let Him into our feelings and emotions. When I think of peace, I think a lot about therapy. I am a huge fan of therapy, so much that I go every single month regardless of how life seems to be panning out. Although he probably could, my therapist isn't solving my problems. Rather, I invite him into my problems. In that, I find peace through self-exploration. And within that, because I'm born again, I find Holy Spirit.

PATIENCE

If you don't grow in patience, you grow impatient. Those are the only two real options. There's not a whole lot of staying where you are when it comes to being okay with waiting. Patience is the key to any success. Spiritual, relational, economical, and professional success are predicated on patience. The space between those who have and those who don't is the same between those who wait and those who hurry.

Of course, there is something about the hustle. But hustling without the patience to see success is hustling toward the edge of a cliff instead of up the mountain. If you have a goal, you have a mountain in front of you. You typically can't change the mountain unless you lower your expectations or standards. Therefore, you must face the mountain and grow with every step you take. We grow in our journey with God through Holy Spirit, especially in seasons of patience. Fruit are grown entirely in patience. You'd never see a fruit farmer yelling at their fruit to grow. They wait and understand there are seasons of waiting and seasons of harvest. When you look at a seed, it doesn't seem like much, but over a generation, it could be an orchard. The best part? You are the seed.

KINDNESS/GOODNESS

I have never seen a kind apple before, but I know I've seen good apples, and that's how I know to buy them. When I go to the grocery store, I always buy Gala apples because any other kind of apple is a pear, and pears are generally gross.

I have found that we often mix the ideas of kindness and goodness. They may be connected, but they have their differences. Kindness is based on the action, while goodness is based on the moral behind the action. A great example is taking out the trash for my wife. Taking out the trash is a kind, considerate act for me to do so that she doesn't have to. Goodness is when I don't feel the need to tell her that I did. Kindness seems to be tied to what is beneficial for others, doing the generous thing. Goodness is doing something positive, what is right, regardless of benefit.

FAITHFULLNESS

Part of faithfulness is being faithful with what you've been gifted to do and with what you are given. Favor and faithfulness have a snowball effect. The more faithful you are, the more favor seems to follow. The most observably faithful people I know are also the most observably favored people I know. It's interesting that, when we choose to do God's will for our lives and believe before we see, faith causes things to shift.

If you aren't faithful, it's hard to be fruitful. The whole premise of faithfulness is based on the idea of continuation. Having a faithful marriage is one that has lasted over time. When you were faithful toward a new job, that means you waited for it. Faithfulness and patience could be siblings.

GENTLENESS

I have heard that gentleness is controlled strength.

The people I have the most respect for end up being the gentlest. Gentle people are those who, when being yelled at, don't yell back. These people have all the power and don't use it. When you are gentle, you end up having all the leverage because you don't fall into what others fall into, which is trying to be something that you usually aren't.

Gentleness and selflessness seem to be interconnected. When you are humble, you naturally become gentle, because the opposite of gentleness would, in many ways, be aggression or pushing your agenda. Gentleness can be the most powerful action in a room of powerful people, because it shows others that you don't need to be powerful to have presence.

SELF-CONTROL

This is what I feel we need the most and want the least. Maybe it's just me. Other translations of the Bible call it "long-suffering." No, thanks. In no way does long-suffering sound good. I'll take self-control any day.

Maybe you can see that the fruit I'm working on the most is self-control, even in my writing, speaking, and other communication. For me, self-control is almost always tied to my communication. When I stop myself from saying what I feel, I start to see where my feelings could be wrong. Self-control is a teacher and keeps us from stepping in or saying the wrong thing at the wrong time. Holy Spirit moves through us, changing us and helping us to have more self-control. The less self-controlled we are, the more out of control our behavior becomes.

Self-control is walking away and keeping your mouth shut even when you have the best comeback. Self-control is often at the core of a good conflict with someone. The more we hang out with Holy Spirit, the more controlled we will be. When He's in control, life is way better anyway. More of God. Less of self.

WHY SHOULD YOU DESIRE THESE?

Besides the obvious that all nine fruits are positive and bring out the best in us and others, there is a great reason to seek out and grow in them. They are what will keep you rooted, not allowing God's hand on your life to outweigh your character. The fruit of Holy Spirit is what creates Godly character within all believers. In my book, *The Holy Spirit Is Not A Bird*, I break down and talk through all the gifts of Holy Spirit. They are amazing and miraculous, but if you don't have any fruit, the miraculous gets rotten really quickly.

The fruit sustains our spiritual life and growth.

HOW TO GROW IN THE FRUIT

When I was growing up, I lived across the street from a tiny farm with all kinds of different foods. Every morning as I waited for the school bus, I would look around at the fields. Occasionally, I would see people working. Sometimes they walked to where nothing was growing yet, as they had only recently planted seeds. While standing in the middle of the dirt, they would look down toward the ground and yell, "Grow! Grow right now!" They would scream every time until they started seeing plants beginning to grow.

Of course, this sounds ridiculous and could have just been a weird dream I was having every now and then. It would be insane for a farmer, whose entire livelihood is based on plants growing so they can sell them and eat them, to yell the plants into existence. But how many times do we do the same thing with the fruit of Holy Spirit?

We grow these fruit in only one way—by hanging out with the one who has the fruit.

REFLECTIONS

What fruit of the Holy Spirit do you feel as if you have the best handle on?

_____

_____

_____

_____

_____

What is one way you can love others better?

_____

_____

_____

_____

_____

How do you feel like you are producing fruit?

_____

_____

_____

_____

_____

BETTER THAN JESUS

Friendship With Holy Spirit

I once heard that the greatest miracle Jesus ever did was have 12 friends, which is hilariously true. More often than not, I'm way more likely to see my glass of water turn into wine than to have 12 friends at the table. Friendship is hard. Real friends, those who are with you in tragedy, who help you when you need it, and who accept your help when they need it, are rare. Friends are hard to come by, and I think that's a huge purpose of Holy Spirit. Holy Spirit is here to lead us into friendship—to show us what friendship, kinship, looks like in the healthiest way possible. There are many synonyms for what Holy Spirit does, or who He is, in our lives: comforter, helper, paraclete, and the one I enjoy most—friend. Better yet, He's my friend. Honestly, He's probably my best friend. Before my friendship with my spouse, childhood friends, or the friends who have gone through tragedy with me, Holy Spirit is a better friend than all of them.

Friendships aren't silent. We must learn to listen and to speak. When I first met my wife, I was just trying to figure out how to speak to her and listen to what she was saying, let alone how she was saying it. On our first date, I was asked three times if we were even on a date. Clearly, I had not communicated that part and was still learning how to speak to her in a way I knew she'd understand what in the world I was saying.

All friendships and relationships, including those we have in the workplace, depend on communication. I would say that every conflict begins with lack of communication or miscommunication. If we slow down, think the best of each other, and pursue getting under the weight of how others feel when we talk to them, we should make it out alright. When we can understand that Holy Spirit isn't just here for us to serve Him but that we can hang out with Him, talk with Him and hear His voice, that elevates everything.

For many, me included, hearing Holy Spirit's voice and making space to do so can be difficult at times. I want to break down how we can have a clearer idea of Holy Spirit's voice. If we can't hear His voice, we'll never have friendship; we'll just have religion.

1. PROBABLY

I'm rarely 100 percent sure about hearing God or feeling any nudges He gives me. I only feel sure once I've already stepped out in faith and seen what He said come to pass. If I thought I knew I'd heard from God, it would most likely have been 100 percent me I'd actually heard. You will be able to say, "This is probably God," which is healthy and normal. The benefit of "probably" is that when you miss it, and you will because we are constantly learning how to commune with Holy Spirit, you get to learn how to hear Him better. Similar to any relationship, no matter the longevity of it, there are always moments when you need clarity on what's being said. "Probably" takes all the pressure off, since we are all constantly learning.

As I am writing this, we are in the middle of the COVID-19 pandemic, and it's hitting the world in different ways. One year ago, way before anyone had any idea of this virus, I was speaking at an event at an amazing church in Oklahoma. At the end of the event, I felt like I had a word for the church, which is not unusual for how we operate at our events. What was unusual was what I felt Holy Spirit prompting me to say. I didn't know if it was Him, but I stepped out and said it: "I feel as if there is going to be a virus of giving that is going to come upon this church." I thought I was speaking to the idea that giving was going to be contagious. An entire year after I gave that word, COVID-19 began to spread and I got a call from the pastor of that church. He shared with me what is going on in their church and all that God is doing. He ended the conversation letting me know that the church received thousands of dollars of relief money due to the virus. He told me that he was talking with God while on a drive, praising Him for all of the provisions in this crazy season, when Holy Spirit spoke to him: "I already told you this was going to happen. Why are you surprised?" In that moment, the pastor remembered the word I'd given, that he'd written down a year prior, about a virus of giving coming to him.

That word from God meant nothing to me, and I remember telling the audience how odd the word "virus" was, but that it was what I felt Holy Spirit wanted me to say. That was my "probably" moment. It took an entire year for Holy Spirit's voice to go from probably to promise. It was totally worth it, not just for me to be encouraged that I hear Holy Spirit, but because Holy Spirit became even more real to a people in Oklahoma because of a "probably" word.

For the record, I have been wrong, too. I will always own those instances, because it is not that God is saying the wrong words—it is how I listen to God that is the miss. "Probably" doesn't give us permission to say whatever we want or do whatever we feel, but it does give us grace to test the waters and find out if a word is from God, as long as it lines up with the pages of His Word.

2. PAGES

There is a good reason to read the Word of God. When

you understand the Word of God and God's character, you can better identify His voice. If you own a Bible and say you haven't heard God's voice in a long time, you've played yourself. You are wrong. God's Word is living and active, attempting to activate you. Your problem might be that you're simply reading the Bible instead of listening to what it says. When you shift your perspective from reading the Bible to taking notice of what it actually says, your view of what you're reading can also change. There are many cliché sayings about how the Bible is the only book that reads you. But this is quite true when you move from looking at it as just another book to viewing it as an avenue for God to speak.

The Word of God is the foundation for all other Godly communication. If you want to build a house but try to start with the roof or the door, you'll never be able to build a stable and healthy home. The Word of God is your foundation for knowing who God is and how you can hear His voice.

3. PEOPLE

Community is a big deal. A friend of mine once said, "Jesus spent His last moments breaking bread with His friends. That's how important community was to Jesus." I've thought about that time and time again. Jesus was getting ready to be betrayed, beaten and tortured to death for us. He didn't call down heaven or go perform a few final miracles before all of this. He spent time with His people, even one of whom was going to cause Him

91

the most pain anyone could ever endure. When Jesus could have been with anyone, doing anything, He was eating dinner with His friends.

We are not meant to do life alone. This is why I love the local church. I travel a lot to speak at conferences and churches. When I am not doing that, I'm sure to be with my own church community, because I don't want to do anything outside of a covering or outside of community. This is the same reason why I want to have friends who hear from God better than I do, have more money than I do, and are better spouses than I am. I want to be surrounded by people who are better than me, so I can gain their wisdom and become a better disciple of Jesus. If you surround yourself with amazing people, you become an amazing person.

I want to hear from God through my friends and with my friends, which is why it's such a big deal to be a part of a local church on a regular basis. You never want to think you heard a word from God but have no one to bounce it off. There is always someone who knows the Word, or God, more than you, so you need to get under a covering with pastors, mentors and counselors to make sure you're on the right path. Of course, this isn't for every single little thing you think of. But those big moments and massive nudges, like to move across the country, are a great time to reach out to a covering and have them pray with you and hear from God, too.

You don't just need community for accountability and

covering. You also need it so you can party when things are amazing and shifting in your life. When your life is down, get around people whose lives are up. God will show you people who are in different places so you can see where you could be someday. God will often bring people into your life for you to recognize what's possible.

4. PRAYER

This is when it gets personal. Prayer is communicating with Holy Spirit like He's in the room, because He is. I talk to Holy Spirit like He is my best friend and, over time, He has become that. Take the pressure off of yourself to have the perfect conversation with God. You're not perfect, so stop behaving like God thinks you need to be. Be real, be yourself. After a while, you'll be able to hear God's voice with more clarity than you hear your friends' voices.

Remember, don't talk to Holy Spirit about what you think you're supposed to talk about. Talk to Holy Spirit about what you actually want to talk about. I remember a time while vacationing in Maui with my wife. We were driving up a mountain with miles of beautiful views and scenery. We drove a total of at least three hours that day, if not more. Three hours of driving isn't the longest we had ever been in transport together, as we've flown around the world on flights as long as 15 hours. The difference between a 15-hour flight to China and a three-hour drive up a mountain is that there are no movies.

BETTER THAN JESUS

It's just us. We did our best not to listen to music much, because we so value the time to talk. Here's the kicker: We didn't plan our conversations. We just talked. We talked about big ideas for our future, family and travels, while, seconds later, talking about the next movie we wanted to see and where to go for dinner. This is what Holy Spirit friendship should look like. Friendship with Him is not about a list of how or what to pray. When you can, and however you can, talk to Holy Spirit about what you really want to talk to Him about. Things happen that wouldn't normally happen when you pray.

UN-THE HOLY SPIRIT

Most people pick up pretty quickly on the fact that I don't say, "The Holy Spirit," but rather, "Holy Spirit." I do this for a couple of reasons, and it's become very beneficial.

First, it just sounds cooler. That might sound petty, but it's the truth. In my opinion, it's a more modern and relevant way to speak to and about Holy Spirit. At the end of the day, Holy Spirit isn't an "it." He has personhood and a personality, so I want to address Him according to that. To me, it sounds better and helps put my sights on His personhood.

I understand that you may have been brought up in a more traditional context, and you may feel more comfortable calling out to Him as "the Holy Spirit." I don't think there's any problem with that. The problem only comes when you are more concerned with what you call Him than what He's calling out in you.

There's nothing like friendship with Holy Spirit, and He earnestly desires for you to participate in it with Him.

REFLECTIONS

If you were to give Holy Spirit a best friend nickname
what woud it be?

_____

_____

_____

_____

_____

Are you having probably moments?

_____

_____

_____

_____

How can you better pursue healthy people in your
friendships?

_____

_____

_____

_____

_____

BETTER THAN JESUS

Having A Miraculous Life

When we understand Holy Spirit's role in our lives, the journey toward a miraculous life should begin. Miracles are anything healthy and positive that wouldn't normally be possible without Jesus. There are financial miracles, which my wife and I have seen again and again. There have been moments when we've sown and reaped more than we could have ever imagined. We've witnessed our friends get a deal on a house that just makes absolutely zero sense. Miracles can also involve someone being instantly healed or healed of an incurable illness. Something as simple, yet complex, as leading someone to Jesus is a miracle—the greatest miracle of all and, really, why miracles exist in the first place. Miracles point people to Jesus. If they point people to you, then there's a problem.

When you think, "That must have been God," it typically was. Miracles might already be happening in your life and you don't even know it. You may think that's crazy; however, we can often miss the miracle because of how we measure. If you're praying for your dream job and don't get it the next day but you get a raise on your current job, receive it. If your marriage isn't where you want it to be but it's progressing, own that.

Having a miraculous life isn't weird. People who think they are the miraculous life … Yeah, that's weird. I realized a while ago that there were times when I would say I wanted to be used by Holy Spirit, but it seemed more like I was using Holy Spirit instead of Him using me. Holy Spirit empowers us, but we have no power without Him. Jesus wants us to be used and to experience miracles. In John 14, Jesus talks about this Himself: "Very truly I tell you, whoever believes in me will do the works I have been doing, and they will do even greater things than these, because I am going to the Father. And I will do whatever you ask in my name, so that the Father may be glorified in the Son. You may ask me for anything in my name, and I will do it." Jesus performed miracles everywhere He went, and we will regularly experience the same when Holy Spirit is within us and upon us. The same Holy Spirit that was in Jesus is within us, empowering us to be conduits of the miraculous. The key to what Jesus says is that miracles happen in His name, by His authority given to us through what He did on the cross and through Holy Spirit. Miracles aren't about us.

They are all about making Jesus more famous.

It's funny how many of my family and friends don't believe God does miracles, at least until they need one. When they get sick, God suddenly becomes more powerful. We hear all the excuses and reasons why they don't believe in the very miracles we see on a regular basis, until they need a miracle of their own.

Most people don't believe in miracles because miracles validate the lack of power in their own lives.

Miracles are for everyone who has given their life to Jesus. For goodness sake, that's a miracle in itself! Every miracle that Jesus does is an expectation that we can have. Jesus tells us that we will do even greater things (greater in number) than these. We are all called into this. There are two categories of miracles that I see take place: the ones we need to see and the ones we want to see.

NEED-BASED MIRACLES

I understand the need for miracles. At this very moment, you probably either need one in your own life or know someone who does. That's okay. Needing miracles isn't inherently a bad thing. It's a human thing. Where it gets a little odd is when we go from not believing to believing, contingent upon whether or not we need one. I know people who not only don't believe but speak against God doing miracles in the modern world. But when diagnosed with chronic illness, they suddenly believe in miracles. What's unhealthy is that many never develop a different set of beliefs. God becomes their backup plan, only calling on Him when they have exhausted their own resources. When we do that, we are choosing to believe in our own power over God's—until we realize ours doesn't actually exist.

There will always be a need for miracles as long we live on the earth, which, due to sin, is a fallen world where sickness, trouble, and negative desperation occurs. When we are born again, when we have Holy Spirit with us and may also experience Holy Spirit upon us, miracles become a natural phenomenon. God is a good heavenly Father and, as the Bible puts it, gives good gifts to His children—gifts that are much better than what we even find in nature. God wants to give us what we need. So, we don't need to beg for miracles. We don't need to beg for what God already wants to give us.

The miracles you need right now—the ones your spouse's parent, your child, or coworker need—are all things God wants to provide. God wants to meet your need. God is good all the time, but He may not move in our timing.

If you need a miracle right now, I'm praying for you and with you as I'm typing this on my computer. I'm praying this season of need will pass. I'm praying you would live and not die, that you would have life, and an abundant one at that. God loves you more than you understand,

and that's okay, too.

WANT-BASED MIRACLES

What if we had the maturity to call on God more than just when we need him? That's real relationship.

I have an acquaintance, or whatever you call someone you don't really like, who I went to college with. The only time I ever hear from him is when he is a part of a new multi-level marketing scheme. He would call this a business, but when you're doing multi-level marketing, you are the business. I get a message from him about every nine months. The message always starts very kind and normal, asking how my life is and apologizing for how long it's been since we've connected. Once I've reached this point in the conversation, I'm always on my toes with expectation that he is simply being a good human and won't make an ask. But wouldn't you know it? Without fail, when I've finished talking about what I'm up to, he has a "great opportunity" for me. I'm positive I make more money than him, so I don't think he understands what a great opportunity is. This is quite satirical to me, which is why I still respond to him. You never know, maybe one of these days I'll hear a pitch that is actually good.

For too many of us, our relationship with Holy Spirit is the same when it comes to miracles. We don't talk to Him until we want to sell some weight loss coffee, essential oils, or lose that extra 20 pounds in 20 days. We've mixed up how this relationship really works. Holy Spirit is the living God of the universe who lives within us. We don't call the shots; we embark on a journey.

I used to want miracles in a really unhealthy way. When I first started seeing miracles happen through me, they were a form of validation. I had this idea that as long as God was using me and miracles were taking place, I was in good standing with Him (which isn't always the case). It got so bad that when I was asked to speak at events, I wouldn't ask God what the people at that event needed. I would deliver messages that gave me the opportunity to pray for the most people just so that I could see miracles. On paper, that isn't terrible, but if miracles take precedence over obedience to God, that's messed up. I had an unhealthy want of miracles, so I had to have a sort of miracle detox in order for my interactions with God to go back to relational rather than transactional.

Pursuing miracles is also unhealthy. We aren't meant to follow after miracles; miracles should follow us. When you chase miracles, signs and wonders, you will lose your faith when you stop seeing them. The healthiest way I know to experience miracles in my life is based on Jesus' example, what I've seen Him doing and how He taught His disciples.

I want to take a look at two instances that involve fishing, which I hate. I hate fishing. Well, let me rephrase that. I love fishing. I just hate the worm and putting it on the hook (which I'm afraid of). I hate touching fish, the smell of fish, and the idea of taking a hook out of a fish all so I can hold the fish for a picture. Yeah, fishing isn't my thing; however, I do weirdly enjoy watching those fishing crew shows for some reason. (I think I'm always waiting for something crazy to happen, like Jaws is going to show up or something.)

FISHING FOR MIRACLES

On one occasion, while the crowd was pressing in on him to hear the word of God, he was standing by the lake of Gennesaret, and he saw two boats by the lake, but the fishermen had gone out of them and were washing their nets. Getting into one of the boats, which was Simon's, he asked him to put out a little from the land. And he sat down and taught the people from the boat. And when he had finished speaking, he said to Simon, "Put out into the deep and let down your nets for a catch." And Simon answered, "Master, we toiled all night and took nothing! But at your word I will let down the nets." And when they had done this, they enclosed a large number of fish, and their nets were breaking. They signaled to their partners in the other boat to come and help them. And they came and filled both the boats, so that they began to sink. But when Simon Peter saw it, he fell down at Jesus' knees, saying, "Depart from me, for I am a sinful man, O Lord." For he and all who were with him were astonished at the catch of fish that they had taken, and so also were James and John, sons of Zebedee, who were partners with Simon. And Jesus said to Simon, "Do not be afraid; from now on you will be catching men." And when they had brought their boats to land, they left everything and followed him. (Luke 5:1-11)

I love this look into where Jesus and Peter's lives collide. It shows us how to prepare for a miracle. Jesus shows up to see fishermen, not men who are fishing but vocational fishermen, whose lives depend on catching fish. They're living their normal lives and, in this case, their fishing isn't going too well. It makes me wonder, "Were they ever good at this?" There's another passage of Scripture in which, after He is raised from the dead, Jesus is helping Peter. Once again, Peter is struggling to catch fish (maybe he just wasn't good at this). Peter ended up being a much better fisher of men than fisherman, and I'm sure he was glad that worked out. I envision Peter writing a letter to his mom after leaving to follow Jesus. After reading the letter, his mom says, "Thank God (get it?), because that fishing for fish job wasn't working out." I also wonder how weird it must have been for Peter to later find out he, a professional fisherman, was given advice from a guy who made chairs for a living …

Let's break down Luke 5:1-11. The fishermen are washing their nets after not catching many fish. Jesus borrows a boat to preach from. He then tells these future disciples to go back out and drop their nets to catch some fish. Peter tells Him they already tried that and didn't catch anything all night long. But because of Jesus' authority, Peter then decides to listen to Him. The fishermen drop the nets and, immediately, the nets fill with so many fish that they begin to break. The future disciples ask other fishermen in a boat near them to help with all the fish. Both boats have so many fish that they start to sink. Peter gets to land, sees Jesus, and repents.

If you think you see miracles all the time, I would ask you how big your net is for receiving them. I have a feeling that some of you keep seeing the nets breaking, but it's because you have a child-sized toy net. We can easily get stuck in one miracle and forget to move on toward the next thing Holy Spirit has for us. You often see the evidence of this when someone constantly shares the same testimony of what God did, but it took place years. or even decades, ago. How crazy would it be if I told you the best meal of my life was on my wedding day? You would think I'm crazy because that was so many years ago. Even more, what if I said our wedding was the best day of our marriage? My wedding was the best day of my marriage for one day. After that, it was the worst day of our marriage because we have been growing in every way ever since. My prayer for every couple on their wedding day is that it would be the worst day of their marriage. I'm not saying that the wedding itself would be bad, but I am praying that every couple grows and has a better marriage every day. The first miracle is the wedding cake, but you can't keep eating years old cake.

We see Peter with his people as they are washing their nets, implying that they are done for the day. Here's a little something: Don't wash your nets before the miracle. Don't give up on the empty net. Nets are made to be filled. Make sure you have nets. If you're believing for a financial miracle, open the savings account. If you're believing for healing, pray a prayer of faith. If you want to find a spouse, then go on a date. These steps don't make these things happen, but there's faith in stepping out and preparing for what God could do.

Jesus borrowing a boat that isn't His is hilarious to me. This is totally something a parent would do. I think we all have one parent or relative who will cut in line but pretend they are meeting friends they know, just so their kids can get ahead in line. For whatever reason, this is how I see Jesus. He sees a boat and gets right in it. (I guess you can do that when you're God.) Jesus teaches from the boat and, after He wraps up His message, He sees Peter and tells him to take his boat and let down the net in deep waters—the very place Peter was all night, the place that is probably reminds him of the failure of the night before. Peter is being asked to go to the place where he failed. So, the failure turns into a lesson. There is no such thing as failure when Jesus is with you.

I realized that if I was Peter, I would feel like I'd failed, too. He has already gone and he's already tired. I've been there. The first thing that comes to my mind is dating. Before I met my wife, I was convinced every girl I dated would be my wife. I'm pretty sure I've told my parents, "She's the one," a dozen times. Okay, maybe not a dozen, because I've only dated, like, three girls, but you get the point. While in each of those three serious relationships, or when simply meeting a girl for coffee, I prayed this crazy prayer. At 15 years old, and for every girl after, I prayed: "God, let this girl be my wife." Can I tell you the best thing about God not answering that prayer? Some of those ladies are straight up crazy. I dodged some bullets like I'm Neo from the Matrix. (If I ever start a rap career, that's going in my album.)

I was desperate for a miracle—what I thought God would want for me, at least. I was fishing and had multiple nets. (They were empty nets, but whatever.) I would date different girls and every time I experienced a breakup, I would be devastated and nearly frustrated with God. Why isn't He answering my prayers? I realized that sometimes God isn't answering my prayers because He has a better prayer for me to pray. Enter Rebecca.

When I met my wife, I never prayed for God to let her be my wife. Why? That had never worked before. But now that I have Holy Spirit in my life, I can hear His voice. I knew Rebecca would be my wife. (Rule of thumb: If you're dating someone and swear that God has told you they're your spouse, don't tell them. That's just weird.) I met Rebecca at a time in my life when, in many respects, I was cleaning my nets since I hadn't caught anything. When Rebecca showed up, I had to go back out and drop the net to see what would happen.

Peter gets back to shore after witnessing a miracle of provision and abundance greater than he had ever seen. This is where many of us stop in our miracle. Once we see it, we are excited and we move on. Peter actually abandons the miracle. The Bible tells us that the other fishermen bring the fish to shore. Peter is so much more amazed by Jesus than the miracle. He brings attention to the reality that Jesus is the miracle. As I write this, I'm tearing up just thinking about that moment. Peter sees the best catch of his life but finds himself caught up in the presence of God. To an extent, he actually pushes Jesus away, because he's aware of his own sin. This is such a great glimpse of humanity. When we sin, we want to push Jesus away, but He's the Savior who pushes and washes away that very sin. Miracles do things to our souls that normal life just can't. They instantly reveal who Jesus is to us, and they reveal us to Jesus.

Miracles lead people to Jesus' feet.

When was the last time you were at His feet?

HOW TO SEE A MIRACLE

If you have never seen a miracle, if you've never experienced one for yourself, today is an awesome day to start allowing Holy Spirit to show you miracles you weren't aware of. He also wants to empower you to have a miraculous marriage, ministry, family, home, finances, and more. You name it. Don't exclude yourself or tell yourself that miracles aren't for you. Miracles can be a part of everyone's life. They may look different from one person to the next, but that's okay.

I am very good at basketball. Let me rephrase that. I am very good at dribbling a basketball. That counts, right? I have never been a very athletic person, but I did play HORSE in my grandparents' driveway when

I was growing up. If you're not familiar with this extreme sport, it involves one person shooting a basket in a particular way, and others have to make the same basket. Otherwise, players get a letter toward the word "HORSE." The first person to spell HORSE is the loser. There's nothing like a game that you only win by watching other people lose. Needless to say, I'm not good at basketball, but I can dribble and play a silly game if I have to. I'd say most people can probably dribble a basketball, and maybe some can even shoot a basket—while others are in the NBA.

I don't support any specific teams, so I'm picking a player based on the fact that I hear his name a lot, even though I have never really seen him play. Let's talk about LeBron. LeBron is one of the best basketball players, one of the best athletes, to ever live. I could play basketball every day of my life, working on it 12 hours a day for 10 years, and I would still look nothing like LeBron when he plays. I would improve, but I would never be able to do what LeBron can do. LeBron doesn't just play basketball. He is gifted to play basketball, and he makes other people want to play basketball. This is what it's like to be gifted in seeing certain miracles.

I have friends who just have God's hand on their lives. Favor follows them. They get every upgrade, free cars, and free houses (that's real), and what's really crazy is that if you know me personally, you won't be able to guess who I'm talking about. I have multiple friends who have this kind of favor over their lives. It's incred-

111

ible. I have friends who hear from God unlike anything I've ever seen. I have counselors, coaches, and pastors in my life who experience God's hand in such unique ways that it makes me want to spend more time with Jesus. None of them play for the NBA. But that's all right with me and with them.

Too often we compare miracles. We see Susie is healed and we aren't, or we see Brad financially blessed in a way that only God could do, and we get bitter. We can even look at our own pasts and be jealous because it seemed like God was moving more then than He is now. Comparison is the thief of our futures and all joy. It's okay that others are gifted in areas you aren't, because you are gifted in areas they aren't. 1 Corinthians 12:4 says that Holy Spirit gives giftings, favor, or whatever you want to call it, when He chooses and to whom He chooses.

Remember when I said that, even if I tried, I couldn't do what LeBron can do? The truth is: LeBron can't do what I can do. I'm okay with that.

Before getting into practical steps, I want to make it easy for you to understand that you can be a part of this. If you're asking the question, "Can I be used in a miraculous way before being baptized in the Holy Spirit?" The answer is, "Of course." Look anywhere in the Bible before Acts 2 for evidence. You got this.

PRACTICAL STEPS FOR SEEING A MIRACLE

1. WRITE/TELL OTHERS ABOUT WHAT YOU'RE LOOKING FOR

Peter's miracle isn't just his. His friends end up filling their boat, too. Miracles are so much more fun when they are experienced with others. Jesus constantly shows us how important community is. In His last moments before being crucified, Jesus wasn't doing another miracle. He was having dinner with His friends, which the Bible calls the Last Supper.

No matter what miracle you're hoping for or in need of, write it down or tell someone about it. This does a couple things: It adds personal accountability, and it starts the faith journey.

2. GO FROM "IF" TO "WHEN"

Your dialogue on the topic needs to shift. If you keep saying, "If God heals me …" or "If God would just …", your dialogue starts to become your belief system. You begin to believe that God's promises are based on if God wants to do them for you, rather than the truth that He does want to save, heal, provide, and do that miracle you need and want. It's not a matter of if but when. Making this change doesn't always mean that the miracle will happen, but it's far better than assuming that it won't.

3. DON'T CHASE THE MIRACLE

When we chase after Jesus, we should naturally see miracles through the power of Holy Spirit. Chasing after miracles typically leads to unhealthy disappointment and a need for God's hand instead of His heart. When we passionately pursue relationship with Holy Spirit, both within us and upon us, then miracles are a natural occurrence. We don't chase miracles; they chase us.

4. PUT IT ALL ON JESUS

The most common mistake we can make is thinking miracles are based on what we can do instead of what Jesus has already done for us. Jesus gave authority to us, to be an extension of Him, so the same Spirit that was in Him now lives in us. When you pray, remember Holy Spirit, the same Holy Spirit that was with Jesus, is within you and can be upon you. When you realize that, the miracles are easy, because you don't do them.

I've seen countless miracles in my life, but I haven't done any of them. It's like having a supernatural credit card with no limit to what it can buy, and you don't have to pay the bill since Jesus already did. We all have the credit card once we have Holy Spirit within us. Jesus did amazing miracles everywhere He went. Now that's our story. *"Greater miracles will you do." (John 14:12)* We aren't naming and claiming; we are claiming what we've been named. We are sons and daughters of God, so let's live like it. As His sons and daughters, we don't have to strive. We step into what God is doing. I think of Jesus' prayer when He tells us to pray, "… your will be done …" We step into what He's doing, not the other way around. We don't name and claim. We step into what God is already claiming.

BUT WHAT IF I DON'T SEE ONE?

I understand the idea that miracles are fun but only for those who are seeing them or who have the potential to. We can easily get messed up emotionally, even spiritually, when we don't see the miracle we've been dying to see. Miracles are always for the glory of Jesus, for Him to be known, so that's the common denominator. In every situation, we need to ask, "Do I want my friend to be healed because they're my friend? Or do I want them to be healed because it will glorify Jesus?"

If you've never seen a miracle, welcome to the club. I hadn't seen a miracle before my own eyes until I was probably 21 years old. If you have a miracle you've been waiting for, keep waiting and keep bringing it to Jesus. If your friend isn't healed or your finances aren't immediately fixed, don't give up. Keep pressing in and keep going after more of who God is. If you're feeling hurt, depressed, or any other emotion tied to your miracle, let Holy Spirit, and other people, into those feelings.

BUT WHAT IF THEY DIDN'T SEE ONE?

When it comes to what can happen when we invite Holy Spirit in, many of us get hurt when we base what can happen on what hasn't happened for others. I think most of us have prayed and fasted for things to take place in other people's lives, and things don't always turn out the way we want them to. People die. People stay sick. They can't have kids. Bankruptcy is declared. Divorce is filed. I totally understand that, at the least, it can be disappointing when we pray and don't see the result we wanted. However, we cannot let what didn't happen for someone else dictate what can happen for others, including ourselves.

I was raised in a home where the working of Holy Spirit in our daily lives wasn't talked about. We were never stretched in our faith for many things. That's not all bad, because it's helped me value what I have now. I haven't allowed what I didn't see in my home growing up to dictate what happens in my home now. If my family of origin didn't believe, that doesn't matter. If my family of origin didn't speak up, that doesn't matter. We aren't our pasts. We aren't the people we used to know, or even the people we know now. We are who we are. Let's invite Holy Spirit into our lives to help us stop trying to compensate for the lack in our pasts. Let's invite Him in to help us reach the abundance of right now.

PRAYER OVER YOU

The first time I really started seeing miracles on a normal basis was when a mentor of mine spoke life into me that it could happen. As I pray over you while I write this, let me do the same for you.

You got this. You are called and chosen by God to do amazing things beyond your wildest dream and highest expectation. Holy Spirit is pursuing you passionately. He wants to use you and do amazing things in you. You will see miracles in your home, relationships, family, children, finances, body, community, and everywhere you go.

Holy Spirit, I call out to you on behalf of my friend reading this right now. Would you go forth and bring life to areas where there has been loss? Bless the parts of my friend where they feel inadequate. Fill my friend with more of who you are, your fruit, and your gifts. May miracles become the norm. May whoever is reading this become the miracle who others in their life need. Help my friend to know that they've got this. Amen.

REFLECTIONS

What fruit of the Holy Spirit do you feel as if you have the best handle on?

_____

_____

_____

_____

_____

What is one way you can love others better?

_____

_____

_____

_____

_____

How do you feel like you are producing fruit?

_____

_____

_____

_____

_____

BETTER THAN JESUS

Get Over Yourself

I've had a pretty wild sports career, from my soccer days on the green team to playing basketball (again, just dribbling) in the driveway growing up. So, try to keep up with my sports analogy, if you can. Mostly anyone can dribble a basketball. I'm not saying you have to be athletic, but I think you can figure out how to do at least that, even if it's only while standing still. Then there are basketball legends who make the game look both easy and impossible at the same time. I've realized that when it comes to being gifted, it's a lot like basketball. Everyone can do something, but not everyone can do anything. I can do something. I can dribble the basketball and maybe play a subpar pick-up game. But I can't do much of anything else when it comes to basketball. We can all think of all-stars who seem to be able to do anything on the court, so much that they make other people want to play the game. People will buy a player's jersey or sneakers based on how good they are. Those are the players who bring value to the game itself.

Being anointed, gifted, having God's hand on your life, or whatever you want to call it, is a lot like this. We can all do certain things because Jesus made a way for us to do them through Holy Spirit's empowerment. Others are gifted in areas that are unexplainable but cause others to want to play the game, wear the jersey, and sport the shoe from the brand deal. The problem comes when we aren't honest with what God has given us. Some of us think the denominator we have is common, and it isn't. It's not equal, and I'm for that. I might not be able to play professional sports, but your kid probably can't either (for the record, little Jimmy isn't going pro). I can't do what some people can, but some people can't do what I can do.

I would love to see people, you reading this, thrive in what God has gifted you and where He has placed His hand on you. Holy Spirit reveals this to us. Let's take the pressure off of ourselves to be someone else, and let's be empowered to be who Holy Spirit is helping us to become.

DISCOVER YOUR UNCOMMON DENOMINATOR

The best way to figure out your uncommon denominator is to have Holy Spirit reveal it through wisdom and prayer. Pray for a moment and ask Holy Spirit to reveal to you what makes you who you are. Where's your uncommon faith placed? What is the thing that you are inordinately blessed at doing? What are you passionate about? Some of us discover this through a passion to do something we've never seen, and it could also come from what we have seen. For example, I have uncommon faith for seeing backs healed. My prayer is that people who have back problems would be healed, even as they read this. I have so much faith for that for two reasons: First, someone prophesied it over me in college. Second, I started seeing it all the time after that. The more you see something, the more you expect it. That might not be common for you, but it is for me. You have things in your life, whether you know it yet or not, that are uncommon faith points that I don't have, and that's amazing.

I've often realized what I'm good at through the revelation of what I'm bad at. This may not matter to you but, personally, I'm not the guy to call up when you're having an issue with demonic stuff going on in your life. I have dealt with it before, but I'm just not that guy. I have one particular friend—that's his thing. He's like a demon hunter. I low-key get nervous around him because I feel like he sees my demons (this is a joke). I've just found through experience that I'm better at praying for things rather than against things. We too often focus on trying to fix what we are bad at when we should double down on what we're blessed at.

YOU MIGHT NEED A NEW MIRROR

A great way to know if someone is good at something is if they aren't the ones talking about it. You ever meet someone who says they are really creative or really pretty? Like, maybe you are, but you might also need a new mirror. So many of us have bent and broken mirrors, so we either see things that aren't there or not enough of what is really there. This is why community is so ridiculously important. Your community can hold up the mirror for you and speak over your life. The more they see you, the more they can see in you. You might not know your gifting because you're not around the type of people who will call it out of you in the best ways. Having a covering, or mentors, is imperative for growth in our relationship with Holy Spirit, because we are accountable to those people. If you say, "Holy Spirit is my covering," or "Holy Spirit is my accountability," you are an idiot. God isn't your accountability partner. He's God. And do you honestly want God to be your accountability? You shouldn't have to have the God of heaven and Earth wake you up when you're surrounded by others to help you. God will judge your actions and Holy Spirit will convict you, but wouldn't it be great to have people in your life who can help you avoid hitting Holy Spirit 's guardrails?

If you don't currently have people in your life who are speaking life into you for today and prophetically over you for your future, you need to start looking out for those people. Don't look for the person who's always trying to give a word; find the people who seem to always have one when you ask them. You can tell Holy Spirit that you want this in your life and follow His guidance to find those people.

YOU MAY BE MORE GIFTED THAN YOU THINK

A thing may be more spiritual when it doesn't look spiritual. I have a friend who is the best salesperson I've seen. He sells stuff I feel no one would pay money for, but the guy makes more than me by a good many paychecks. We are both gifted but if we traded, his gift wouldn't be a gift to me; it'd be a burden.

I'm about to preach. You might be jealous of someone, but if you had their gift, it would become a burden. You aren't made to be underneath the weight of someone else's anointing.

You might be reading this book and, most likely, you don't work with churches for a living like me. You work in the normal world, which is great. Predominately, our giftings are not for the church but what's outside of it. What I'm trying to say is that you don't want my life. You want yours, or at least yours when it's in Holy Spirit's hands.

If you're not gifted to be a prophet, that's fine. If you are gifted to be a prophet, don't be a weirdo.

YOU ARE NOT A PROPHET

During many events I get to be a part of when teaching on Holy Spirit, or praying for people who need healing, there is always, without fail, at least one person who comes up to me and tells me how gifted they are. Can I be honest? If you have to say you're gifted, you're not.

The thing that grinds my gears (yeah, I just went there) is when someone introduces themselves by a title and not their name. "I'm prophet Greg Whoever ..." Bro, please don't be that guy. I preach, prophesy, and pray for a living, and my name hasn't changed. Your title is your lowest level of influence. Seriously, friend, no one cares about your title except you and your mom.

I go to a barber about every three to four weeks. He speaks almost no English and yet, somehow, I feel like we're best friends. (This could be because I tip well, which seems to help that friendship.) Anyway, when I first found out about him, I didn't start going to him because he talked about how much of a good barber he is (not that I would've understood him anyway). I went because I had seen photos of what people looked like after they'd gone to him. The evidence of his gift is in the results of the people who encounter him. At the end of the day, my barber doesn't talk about how good he is because he doesn't have to. (It would actually make the experience worse.) Be like my barber.

We don't need to go around telling others how great we are. Instead, we should be letting people know how great our heavenly Father is—the one who has changed everything about us. If anything else, we should be telling others how great they are. This is why every time my wife and I fly, which is often, the people we thank most aren't the pilots but the people cleaning the bathrooms and taking out the trash. We want to speak life into those who might not love their lives.

If you are naturally or spiritually gifted in a specific area, then great. Shut up and get work done for the Kingdom of God. You're not a prophet. You're just Kevin. This is why I always ask to be introduced using only my name at speaking engagements. I'm not your prophet, pastor, bishop, or whatever. I'm your friend, Ty. At the end of the day, when I am with the Father in heaven, He's only going to call me by my name, not my title of authority, because it's not mine anyway.

Just be you. It's better that way.

You got this.

REFLECTIONS

What do you consider to be your uncommon denominator?

_____

_____

_____

_____

_____

Is there anyone you're jealous of that you need to give to God?

_____

_____

_____

_____

_____

BETTER THAN JESUS

More Than Before

I want to share with you a story to wrap up this book, and I want to be very honest in saying that this doesn't normally happen. What I'm about to share is an experience that could only be God. My wife and I had just finished eating at one of our favorite restaurants. We were really full—we-should-have-worn-sweatpants full. As we were heading home, I experienced what could have only been a sign from God. I want to describe it to you as best as I can remember it. We were driving and, all of a sudden, I saw a sign. It appeared to be a white sign with bright red letters. I was able to read the words on the sign, and I'll never forget what I felt when reading it.

"Hot Now. Krispy Kreme Doughnuts."

I mean, if that's not Holy Spirit speaking, I don't know what is.

If you're not familiar, Krispy Kreme Doughnuts is a nationwide chain specializing in glazed doughnuts. You can even see doughnuts being made at their locations. I remember visiting when I was younger. It was a huge experience watching the whole process then being handed a hot glazed doughnut. It's honestly one of the best tasting things in life.

So, this sign is actually on quite a lot. It's on every time they're selling fresh, hot doughnuts. My wife and I have a couple rules in our marriage, and one of the most important ones is: If the hot sign is on, we go in. So, we did. We had just eaten a large meal and were really full but, come on, they were fresh doughnuts! Doughnut prices are odd because you can buy one for a dollar, or a dozen for less than ten dollars. We always want to be wise with our money. So, we bought a dozen. Somewhere in our heads, that makes more sense, even though it's really terrible for us because we can end up quickly eating them all.

We were full after our meal but when we saw that "Hot Now" sign, we lost our fullness and became hungry for hot doughnuts. I don't think you quite understand, though. We were completely full, as in not-another-bite full. Yet we bought a box of doughnuts and had one each during the drive home. Isn't it crazy how we can go from full to hungry just because we saw a sign?

I want to offer you value at the end of this book by guiding you along the journey to being hungry for more of what Holy Spirit has for you, forever.

HOW WE GET HUNGRY

From what I have found and experienced in my own life, there are two distinct ways to get hungry for more of God (and actual doughnuts from time to time).

But before you get hungry, you have to decide what you will do with your hunger. Will you pursue it and be full to the point of filling others? Or will you let the hunger pass and hope it comes back around?

There are two ways we get hungry: when we go without food and when we get around it.

WITHOUT FOOD

"I'm starving," is a phrase I say all the time, but I have never truly known what it is like to starve. I have never had to wonder where food was going to come from, and I'm aware that isn't everyone's normal. Anytime I have been on a mission trip, fasted for longer than a day, or even worked out for a while, I feel the food I'm missing. The hunger begins to set in. Because I've had a lack of food or no food at all for a certain amount of time, my desire for food becomes very real.

We can all get like this at times, and I don't think it's intentional by any means. Rather, it's what happens when we aren't intentional. I don't think we wake up and think to ourselves, "You know what? Today is a great day to not spend time with God." Right? No matter what level of faith you're on, that would be strange to me.

How we do solve this? We feed ourselves.

This isn't a time when we complain about our church "not feeding us" because it's not a church's job or a pastor's job to give you what you need to survive for a week. That's up to you. The church and its leaders are there to support you and kickstart you into the next week and season of your life. If you told me that you were going to take one big breath and run a mile with only that one breath, I would think you are crazy. You wouldn't make it more than a couple of feet before you'd need to breathe. Yet we do this so often when it comes to reading the Word of God (the Bible), prayer, and community. We can think that once a week (if that) will get us through to the end of the week. If you want a healthy relationship, that just isn't the case. If I treated my spouse the same way you might be treating God, my marriage probably wouldn't last, no matter how seriously we are holding our vows.

If you're starving or feel like you are hungry for more of God because it's been awhile since He's really been in your life, don't be discouraged. Be encouraged. You've got this. God wants to have relationship and spend time with you. That's why He sent Holy Spirit. Jesus is so passionate about you that He died for you and sent Holy Spirit to dwell within you, so that He is always with you and you with Him. Even if you feel lonely right now, know that you are never alone.

AROUND FOOD

You can judge me all you want, but don't pretend you wouldn't go into any doughnut shop that was selling hot doughnuts. I feel like doughnuts are what's going to bring about world peace. All world leaders sit down when there are wars and rumors of wars, and a random country's leader stands up and says, "I brought doughnuts." The other world leaders look around at each other and call a truce, and there you have it. If I was a politician, many of my strategies would involve doughnuts. If the press asked me a hard question, I'd just pull out a box of doughnuts and offer one. This might be my best idea yet. You know why it would work in my fictional future? Because everyone loves to eat when they're around good food.

I think Thanksgiving is the prime example of what happens when we get around food. The whole idea of Thanksgiving is that you fly or drive across the country to spend time with family you probably bicker with. But you know that at the end of the day, there's going to be good food, so you show up. Jesus Himself was basically eating all the time. If I could multiply food, I would never leave my house. The fact that Jesus could multiply

135

food but still chose to leave His home may be the greatest miracle He ever did.

When we get around people who are seeking God, something changes in the atmosphere. We can often feel it. There's something about another person's hunger that can encourage ours. This is why I love the local church. We can be hungry together. We can gather around the table, fill ourselves, and still be hungry when we leave.

MORE THAN BEFORE

Holy Spirit doesn't shame us, but He may convict us into a higher level of living. This can be a good time to reflect on how hungry you are. If you're starving or wanting seconds, Holy Spirit wants to give you more. There is always more than before.

Jesus told us that it's better that He leaves so we can have Holy Spirit within us and upon us. This wasn't a message just for the disciples over 2,000 years ago. This is a message for all believers in Jesus right now. This isn't just "taste and see" (Psalm 34:8). It's "taste and see"— and keep tasting and keep seeing. Holy Spirit was sent by God the Father, as promised, so that every time we hunger and thirst for more, we can be filled.

You got this.

REFLECTIONS

What are you hungry for Holy Spirit to do in your life?

_____

_____

_____

_____

_____

_____

_____

_____

_____

_____

_____

_____

_____

_____

_____

_____

_____

_____

_____

_____

BETTER THAN JESUS

ABOUT THE AUTHOR

Ty Buckingham is inordinately passionate about helping people understand biblical truths in the most simplistic way possible, both as an author and speaker. He has traveled around the world, preaching and teaching with an unassuming personality and speaking style that make it simple and straightforward for anyone to receive from God.

Married to Rebecca, they currently reside in the great state of Georgia. Together, they have seen countless people saved, healed and filled with the Holy Spirit in services and in public. They believe that everyone they meet should have the opportunity to have a genuine encounter with Holy Spirit (without any weird baggage).

TYBUCKINGHAM.COM